"When the Lord cov[ers himself, he is reveal]ing less than himself. [...we see more of him] when we consider the [glory of the Trinity....] *God* offers us a remarkably clear view of our beautiful God as taught in the Holy Scriptures and summarized in the ancient creeds. The pastor-theologians who authored this God-glorifying book beckon us to draw near to the Father through the Son in and by the Spirit. And in so doing, we begin the blessed business of heaven."

—**Joel R. Beeke**, chancellor and professor of systematic theology and homiletics, Puritan Reformed Theological Seminary

"In the era of the Nicene debates, theologians like Gregory of Nazianzus and Augustine of Hippo developed the doctrine of the Trinity and proclaimed it in dogmatic sermons. In the last century, many theologians have worked to retrieve the Nicene doctrine, but few have worked to retrieve Nicene proclamation. Thankfully, this refreshing book and its theologically substantive, pastoral sermons show the untapped potential of the retrieval of the genre of dogmatic preaching, and it calls others to follow suit in preaching the triune God."

—**Glenn Butner**, associate professor of theology and Christian ministry, Sterling College

"The Protestant Reformers loved the church fathers. The Reformers reproduced the best of patristic content on theology proper without reproducing their errors on salvation and the church. In *Proclaiming the Triune God* orthodox trinitarian theology shows itself to be something that can be preached by local pastors and understood by church members. We owe our thanks to the authors because they help readers understand more of what God has revealed of himself. What more can we ask of a Christian book?"

—**Mark Dever**, pastor, Capitol Hill Baptist Church, Washington, DC

"The entirety of the Christian life can be summed up in this: communion with the triune God and his people. In *Proclaiming the Triune God*, these two truths are front and center: The only God who saves is the triune God. And it is the greatest delight of God's people to not just be saved by him but to fellowship with God the

Father, God the Son, and God the Holy Spirit. I am praying more churches will experience a renewed vision of the God who saves and communes with his people."

—**J. T. English**, pastor, Storyline Church, Denver, Colorado

"*Proclaiming the Triune God* sets forth, with scriptural fidelity, theological clarity, and great beauty, a feast of the sublime truth that we worship one God in three persons. This book takes readers on a deep dive into doctrine but makes it accessible to the person in the pew without sacrificing truth. If you want to know and worship our triune God with greater knowledge, devotion, and love, this is the book to read."

—**J. V. Fesko**, Harriet Barbour Professor of Systematic and Historical Theology, Reformed Theological Seminary, Jackson, Mississippi

"Many Christians today treat the doctrine of the Trinity as if it were something largely for academia and not the pulpit or the Christian life. But this has left the church with perhaps its greatest problem: by neglecting the deep things of the faith, we are being left in the shallows. This book proves instead that theology stretches the mind and enlarges the heart in wonder, love, and praise. Here is theology that leads to doxology—to the most deeply transformative delight in the unfathomable gloriousness of the triune God."

—**Michael Reeves**, president and professor of theology, Union School of Theology

"This helpful overview of trinitarian theology began as sermons, and while the authors don't hold back on doctrinal details, they give special attention to why theology matters for the spiritual lives of all believers. I can think of several books that vault up into the doctrine and expertly carry out maneuvers worth applauding, but very few that make sure to stick the landing. High points for this undertaking."

—**Fred Sanders**, professor of theology, Torrey Honors College, Biola University

PROCLAIMING *the* TRIUNE GOD

PROCLAIMING
the
TRIUNE GOD

*The Doctrine of the Trinity
in the Life of the Church*

MATTHEW BARRETT,
RONNI KURTZ,
SAMUEL G. PARKISON
and JOSEPH LANIER

B&H
ACADEMIC®
BRENTWOOD, TENNESSEE

Proclaiming the Triune God: The Doctrine of the Trinity in the Life of the Church
Copyright © 2024 by Matthew Barrett, Ronni Kurtz, Samuel G. Parkison, Joseph Lanier

Published by B&H Academic®
Brentwood, Tennessee

All rights reserved.

ISBN: 978-1-0877-8516-5

Dewey Decimal Classification: 231
Subject Heading: TRINITY \ CHRISTIANITY--DOCTRINES \ GOD

Unless otherwise noted, all Scripture quotations are taken from the *Christian Standard Bible*®. Copyright © 2017 by Holman Bible Publishers. Used by permission. Christian Standard Bible® and CSB® are federally registered trademarks of Holman Bible Publishers.

Scripture quotations marked ESV are taken from *The Holy Bible, English Standard Version*. ESV® Text Edition: 2016. Copyright © 2001 by Crossway Bibles, a publishing ministry of Good News Publishers.

The web addresses referenced in this book were live and correct at the time of the book's publication but may be subject to change.

Cover design by Darren Welch Design.
Illustration sourced from ilbusca/iStock.

Printed in the United States of America

29 28 27 26 25 24 VP 1 2 3 4 5 6 7 8 9 10

To the saints of Emmaus Church,
who heard these sermons preached in 2021.
Few privileges compare to pilgriming with you.

Therefore we wait for you to set in motion these timid first steps of our undertaking, to confirm it so that it may make progress, and to call us into fellowship with the Spirit who guided the prophets and apostles, so that we may apprehend their words in no other sense than that in which they spoke them, and explain the proper meanings of the words according to the realities they signify. For we shall be speaking of what they preached in mystery. . . . Grant us therefore, precision of words, light of understanding, honorable speech, and true faith. Enable us to believe that which we also speak, so that we may confess you one God our Father, and one Lord Jesus Christ as taught by the prophets and apostles.

Hilary of Poitiers, *On the Trinity*, Book 1

CONTENTS

Acknowledgments xiii
Introduction 1

Chapter One   **A Rediscovery** 17
The Centrality of Trinitarian Theology

Chapter Two   **The Saving Trinity** 47
Triune Self-Revelation and the Gospel

Chapter Three   **One God in Trinity** 71
Divine Simplicity in Trinitarian Perspective

Chapter Four   **The Son and His Father** 97
Eternal Generation

Chapter Five   **The Lord and Life-Giver** 125
The Procession of the Holy Spirit

Chapter Six   **Communion with the Undivided Trinity** 151
Inseparable Operations

Conclusion 179
Appendix: The Creeds in the Life of the Church 185
Selected Bibliography 195
Subject Index 207
Scripture Index 219

ACKNOWLEDGMENTS

There is an embarrassment of riches behind this book. The list of folks who deserve mention is longer than any brief acknowledgement section could hold. First, as you will read in the introduction, this book is the product of a sermon series which took place at Emmaus Church in North Kansas City, Missouri. Our first thanks are to the members of Emmaus Church, who heard these sermons preached in 2021. More than a mere church to attend, you all were a people to which we belonged. The privilege of doing covenantal life with you is more than we deserve, and it was the joy of a lifetime to march toward the Promised Land with you all. We would also like to thank Joshua Hedger and Adam Sanders, both elders who did not preach in this sermon series on the Trinity but who, nevertheless, helped shape our thoughts and gave feedback throughout. It was a joy to pastor *with* you and be pastored *by* you.

Next, we would like to acknowledge the capable and erudite team at B&H Academic. Kristen Padilla, Michael McEwen, and Madison Trammel have been a gift to us four. It is not lost on us how important it is to have gifted editors and supportive publishers in your corner, and these three have proven to be that and more.

Finally, we would like to acknowledge our families. Our wives: Elizabeth Barrett, Kristen Kurtz, Kristen Lanier, and Shannon

Parkison, not only supported our ministry at the local level in Emmaus Church, but their support continued as we had the desire to make this study available to a larger audience through this publication. You four are some of the clearest proofs we have of James 1:17, that God is the Father of lights who gives good gifts, much better gifts than we deserve. Between the four of us, there are a number of children represented whom we would like to thank as well: Cassandra, Georgia, Charlie, Lorelei, Finley, Cohen, Ingrid, Titus, George, Jonah, Henry, Lewis, and a Parkison on the way. We pray that you all grow to love and treasure the triune God.

May this book be even a small contribution in bringing orthodox trinitarian theology into the local church, which is the proper location of theology to begin with. May the pages you hold in your hand cause you to delight in our triune God and turn your mind's eye toward contemplating his beauty.

Matthew Barrett
Ronni Kurtz
Joseph Lanier
Samuel G. Parkison

Kansas City, MO
Dayton, OH
Raleigh, NC
Abu Dhabi, UAE

January 2024

INTRODUCTION

This book is born out of two convictions. First, an orthodox doctrine of the Trinity is foundational to the Christian faith. It is not an optional add-on, nor is it a technical matter reserved for those initiated into specialization. Without an orthodox doctrine of the Trinity, there is no Christianity. So, the first conviction is that the stakes are high with the doctrine of the Trinity: it is a nonnegotiable foundation. Second, the doctrine of the Trinity is *for the whole church*. We do not believe that the doctrines described and codified in the creeds and confessions of the Christian tradition are exclusively for academicians and professional theologians. We would reject, therefore, the all-too-common insistence that a classical theistic doctrine of the Trinity—insisting on ostensibly esoteric features like the doctrine of divine simplicity, inseparable operations, eternal generation, and so on—is out of reach for the laity. Classical trinitarianism *preaches* because we have been created and redeemed to participate and enjoy communion with the holy Trinity. These two convictions coalesced to inspire a seven-part sermon series, which was subsequently and heavily edited, rewritten, and arranged into the volume you now hold in your hands.[1]

---

[1] The introduction, along with chapters 1, 5, and 6 were originally drafted by Samuel Parkison; chapter 2 and some of the appendix by Joseph

At the time these sermons were prepared and preached, all four of their authors were pastors at Emmaus Church in North Kansas City, Missouri. These sermons were preached to an average church in the Midwest. The original listeners were not conditioned for austerity or sophisticated lectures. They came week after week to worship with God's people on the Lord's Day, to hear from God's Word, and to live out their Christian lives in very ordinary ways. While it is not uncommon for theologians to receive the criticism that a classical doctrine of the Trinity is too complicated for the average Christian, we (as well as those members of Emmaus Church who heard those sermons preached in 2021) beg to differ.

This book pushes back against the impulse to water down trinitarian doctrine in a reductionistic way for the pew. It is therefore appropriate to place this resource within the same category as other recent works aimed at the lay Christian. We rejoice greatly over the wave of trinitarian books published in the last decade, during which time we have benefited from the erudite and wonderful publications from able theologians.[2]

Lanier; the conclusion, chapter 4, and the appendix by Ronni Kurtz, and chapter 3 by Matthew Barrett. Each author subsequently worked through every chapter with careful editorial attention. The final product is a true "joint statement," written by all four authors.

[2] The following books are for more advanced readers: D. Glenn Butner Jr., *Trinitarian Dogmatics: Exploring the Grammar of the Christian Doctrine of God* (Grand Rapids: Baker Academic, 2022); Fred Sanders, *The Triune God*, New Studies in Dogmatics (Grand Rapids: Zondervan, 2016); Fred Sanders and Scott R. Swain, eds., *Retrieving Eternal Generation* (Grand Rapids: Zondervan, 2017); Scott R. Swain, *The Trinity and the Bible: On Theological Interpretation* (Bellingham, WA: Lexham, 2021); Thomas Joseph White, *The Trinity: On the Nature and Mystery of the One God* (Washington, DC: Catholic University of America Press, 2022);

The kind of work we aspire to be a part of in theological retrieval of historic Christian truths is multiform by necessity. Until recently, most of this work has appropriately operated in the arena of academia. As for *this volume*, we hope to add another contribution to the growing list of books on our triune God with the slight variant that this particular book is meant to encourage the average church member, not the academic theologian. In that way, it could be thought of as a companion to trinitarian volumes aimed to aid the piety and theology of the laity such as Scott R. Swain's *The Trinity: An Introduction,* Matthew Barrett's *Simply Trinity: The Unmanipulated Father, Son, and Spirit,* Phillip Cary's *The Nicene Creed: An Introduction*, or Brandon D. Smith's *The Biblical Trinity: Encountering the Father, Son, and Holy Spirit in Scripture.*[3]

These chapters did originate as homilies, after all. They were spiritual meals prepared to feed the souls of God's people, and they should be read in that same spirit. Yet this does not mean that we shrink back from instruction. Indeed, these chapters may *stretch* the reader (just as they stretched their listeners). We are unembarrassed by this and consider it a feature, not a bug. A "doxologically doctrinal" sermon or book chapter is no oxymoron. In fact, it is downright inappropriate to have doxology without doctrine, and vice versa.

R. B. Jamieson and Tyler R. Wittman, *Biblical Reasoning: Christological and Trinitarian Rules for Exegesis* (Grand Rapids: Baker Academic, 2022).

[3] Scott R. Swain, *The Trinity: An Introduction* (Wheaton, IL: Crossway, 2021); Matthew Barrett, *Simply Trinity: The Unmanipulated Father, Son, and Spirit* (Grand Rapids: Baker, 2021); Brandon D. Smith, *The Biblical Trinity: Encountering the Father, Son, and Holy Spirit in Scripture* (Bellingham, WA: Lexham, 2023); Phillip Cary, *The Nicene Creed: An Introduction* (Bellingham, WA: Lexham, 2023).

Dogmatic and *Biblical?*

This brings us to two more important features we wish to point out about these chapters. First, these chapters are dogmatic and lean heavily on the historic Christian tradition. As sermons, they were intended to make their listeners *catholic* (with a small *c*, as in "universal"). These chapters are unabashedly creedal, standing on the shoulders of pastors and theologians who have contemplated—and have codified their contemplations of—the doctrine of the Trinity. They drive against the "chronological snobbery" that would lead us to believe that modern ways of thinking are better simply *because* they are modern.[4] This is an important point to dwell on because our age is a rapidly moving one. Often, we are those who are historically detached and sometimes even predisposed to devaluing tradition. This can lead to a kind of uprootedness, in which we are left afloat without a proper embrace of heritage. This state of affairs, of course, is not unique to the world of theology alone—it is a feature of late modernity, and all of us without exception (the authors of this present volume included) cannot help but breathe the air of our own day. The question is not whether we will *opt into* a modern way of thinking disparagingly about the past, but rather whether we will *opt out* of it.

Some may consider this detached vantage point an asset of the twenty-first century and not a burden, as if the institutions and beliefs of yesteryear are shackles which we should consider ourselves fortunate to leave behind. However, far from living in liberty, the historically unrooted Christian does not actually know what he is missing. He is like the man G. K. Chesterton describes as "the ill-educated Christian turning gradually into the

---

[4] See C. S. Lewis, *Surprised by Joy* (London: Geoffrey Bles, 1955), 139.

ill-tempered agnostic, entangled in the end of a feud of which he never understood the beginning, blighted with a sort of hereditary boredom with he knows not what, and already weary of hearing what he has never heard."[5] Over and against this disposition the contributors of this volume consider the creeds and confessions of the Christian traditions to be wings that put the soul to flight. We find the heritage we have received from the saints before us to be a gift, a gift which we hope to explore throughout the pages of the book.

Second, these chapters are "biblical," but not in the sense that this term often connotes. We aim for this volume to move beyond more simplistic formulations of the doctrine in which a Christian understanding of the trinity is merely collecting and adding up isolated references, as if the doctrine of the Trinity could be boiled down to a mathematical calculation (passages about the Father + passages about the Son + passages about the Spirit = the doctrine of the Trinity).[6] These chapters rather commend a more contemplative examination of the Scriptures. In these pages, we do not merely permit but rather positively encourage our readers to look at the Scriptures *with trinitarian lenses*. We both explore the biblical rationale of the historic creeds and confessions (i.e.,

---

[5] G. K. Chesterton, *The Everlasting Man* (1925; repr., Moscow, ID: Canon, 2021), 5.

[6] Such an approach could be called *naïve* biblicism, and it should be distinguished from being biblical. Being biblical was the approach of the Reformers, but *naïve* biblicism was the approach of the Radicals, who lived and wrote during the same period and who justified their departure from historic orthodoxy on "biblical" grounds. This would include groups like the Anabaptists and more extreme heresies like Socinianism. To understand what defines biblicism, see Matthew Barrett, *The Reformation as Renewal: Retrieving the One, Holy, Catholic, and Apostolic Church* (Grand Rapids: Zondervan Academic, 2023), 21.

tracing out how our faithful forefathers worked their way from the Scriptures to the creeds) and examine the Scriptures with creedal and confessional glasses. Thus, we are commending a particular kind of theological methodology, one that involves *contemplation* as a key component.

What exactly does this mean? In his book, *Contemplating God with the Great Tradition: Recovering Trinitarian Classical Theism*, Craig A. Carter describes this approach as *second exegesis*. For Carter, the task of a theologian certainly includes that crucial work of coming straight to the text of Scripture, reading it in all its historical and grammatical and literary and canonical context, and then drawing conclusions from that reading about what must be true of God and reality. Unlike many popular conceptions of the interpreter's task, however, Carter insists that the work of exegesis is not yet brought to completion at this point. Once those initial implications are considered, the theologian is now responsible for *contemplating* God in light of these findings and to thereby draw new findings in the light of general revelation and natural theology. The theologian would be shortsighted to insist on practicing contemplation in isolation from Christianity's great tradition and heritage. Further, this act of contemplation is no mere methodological step; it is a *spiritual* discipline: "The kind of contemplation I have in mind here is prayerful contemplation," says Carter, "that is, contemplation undertaken in the presence of God."[7] After having engaged in this rich work of contemplation, the theologian is prepared to begin the process of *second* exegesis, wherein he reengages the text in light of said contemplation, and thereby interrogates

---

[7] Craig A. Carter, *Contemplating God with the Great Tradition: Recovering Trinitarian Classical Theism* (Grand Rapids: Baker Academic, 2021), 260.

what he has discovered. We try to demonstrate this process in the chapters contained in this volume.

Some evangelicals may be concerned that we are encouraging mere dependence on creedal formulations for exegesis and preaching, but they should not be. Such a concern is understandable. If evangelicals are anything, they are a *Bible people*—people of the Book who hold the Holy Scriptures as sufficient and authoritative. This is undoubtedly a good thing. But must this high view of Scripture lead to a depreciated view of the church's historic creeds? It would be a mistake to answer this question in the affirmative. While the Scriptures are authoritative and sufficient in their own right, they still must be interpreted. The creeds have functioned as faithful interpretations of the Scriptures—well-forged articulations of the faith once for all delivered to the saints. The creeds are the collected wisdom of Christ's church, and confessing them is a way for evangelicals today to take Christ at his word when he promised that he would build his church and that the gates of hell would not prevail against it. When we read and confess the ancient creeds, we are self-consciously identifying ourselves with our family history. We believe that standing on the faithful foundation of those who have gone before us is one of the best ways to guard the deposit of faith entrusted to us (cf., Jude v. 3) from interpretations of the biblical text that lead the church into heresy. The creeds and confessions and dogmatic categories to which we introduce our readers, in other words, should not be seen as something separated or disconnected from the task of reading the Bible. We believe, rather, that the historic language of orthodox trinitarianism *helps* us read the Bible more fruitfully.

Therefore, in these chapters, we incorporate historical theology with intention, not as a detraction from the Scriptures, but as a faithful reading of the Scriptures. We look at the text, and we invite great theologians from the church catholic to sit down next to us and look at the text with us. As Christians, we are not intended to read the Bible by ourselves but *with the church.* Therefore, we will introduce historic terminology like "eternal processions" and "modes of subsistence" and "inseparable operations," and we will define these terms and explain why they matter. And in all of this, we labor to do what the creeds do: we labor to preserve and provoke *doxology.* We do not attempt to explain the incomprehensible nature of our triune God, for to explain the unexplainable nature of God is to explain it *away.* No, rather than trying to dispel the mystery, we preserve the mystery with language that is fitting for the sake of rightful worship. We agree with Stephen Charnock when he says, "Though we cannot comprehend him as he is, we must be careful not to fancy him to be what he is not."[8] This is a profoundly *Christian* impulse. For the one who fears God, the desire to praise him with language and thinking that honors him is instinctually attractive.

Psalm 24: An Illustrative Case Study

Consider, for example, how the doctrine of "inseparable operations" (the doctrine that affirms that since the Trinity is undivided, the external operations of the Trinity are also undivided) helps us understand a passage like Psalm 24. R. B. Jamieson and Tyler R. Wittman helpfully summarize this doctrine as a rule for biblical interpretation: "Scripture sometimes attributes to only one divine person a perfection, action, or name common to all three, because of some contextual fit or analogy between the common attribute

---

[8] Stephen Charnock, *The Existence and Attributes of God* (1853; repr., Grand Rapids: Baker, 1979), 1:197.

and the divine person in question. *Read such passages in a way that does not compromise the Trinity's essential oneness and equality.*"[9] How does this help us understand Psalm 24? It helps us make sense of the transition from verse 6 to verse 7, the final section of the psalm. The entire psalm reads:

> The earth and everything in it,
> the world and its inhabitants,
> belong to the Lord;
> for he laid its foundation on the seas
> and established it on the rivers.
>
> Who may ascend the mountain of the Lord?
> Who may stand in his holy place?
> The one who has clean hands and a pure heart,
> who has not appealed to what is false,
> and who has not sworn deceitfully.
> He will receive blessing from the Lord,
> and righteousness from the God of his salvation.
> Such is the generation of those who inquire of him,
> who seek the face of the God of Jacob. *Selah*
>
> Lift up your heads, you gates!
> Rise up, ancient doors!
> Then the King of glory will come in.
> Who is this King of glory?
> The Lord, strong and mighty,
> the Lord, mighty in battle.
> Lift up your heads, you gates!
> Rise up, ancient doors!

---

[9] Jamieson and Wittman, *Biblical Reasoning*, 106; emphasis added.

> Then the King of glory will come in.
> Who is he, this King of glory?
> The Lord of Armies,
>   he is the King of glory. *Selah* (Ps 24:1–10)

Consider the shape of this psalm. After reveling in the sovereign dominion and power of God (vv. 1–2), David asks, "Who may ascend the mountain of the Lord? Who may stand in his holy place?" (v. 3). It is as if he asks, "If *this* is the kind of God our God is, who could possibly stand in his holy presence?" His answer is, "The one who has clean hands and a pure heart, who has not appealed to what is false, and who has not sworn deceitfully" (v. 4). If this is the one who may enter into the Lord's holy place, must we not despair of hope that any man will enter in? The effect of this verse reminds us of John's experience in Revelation 5. It is as if we are with him; we have heard a mighty angel proclaiming with a loud voice, "Who is worthy to open the scroll and break its seals?" and have seen that "no one in heaven or on earth or under the earth was able to open the scroll or even to look in it" (5:2–3). And we, like John, feel despair. But in this state of despair, verses 7–10 hit us with great surprise.

Having asked and answered the question of who may ascend the hill of the Lord to stand in his holy place, it is as if, to our great astonishment, we hear the trumpet blast and the cranking of giant cogs, as the gates of heaven slowly open to welcome the arrival of *Someone. Surely*, we thought, *these gates will never open, for no one has clean hands and a pure heart; everyone at least sometimes appeals to what is false.* And yet, there they open to welcome the victorious procession of One who must meet this description. Who is this One who has clean hands and a pure heart? "The Lord, strong and mighty, the Lord, mighty in battle. . . . The Lord of Armies, he is the King of glory" (Ps 24:8, 10). Those capital letters in your Bible, "L-o-r-d," are the translator's clue to you that the word being translated is the God of Israel's covenant name, Yahweh—the personal, covenantal name that God gave to his chosen people. So, who may ascend the hill of Yahweh? Yahweh himself. The Lord, having apparently descended somehow, now ascends his own hill to stand in his own holy place. We insist that this passage speaks of *Jesus* himself.

Are we justified by the text to draw such conclusions? Is this just another example of theologians trying to squeeze Christ into every text? Or do the Scriptures themselves provide a rationale for seeing Christ fulfill the hopes of this psalm? While there are several textual clues to which we could point to justify this reading, consider the placement of these two movements together. David extols the glory of Yahweh, the Creator of the world, asks the question, "Who may ascend the mountain of [Yahweh]?," and then goes on to describe *Yahweh* coming in! The fact that David envisions the royal procession of Yahweh as the King entering into those "ancient gates" immediately after posing the question of who can ascend the hill of Yahweh to stand in his holy presence, shows that David himself knew that ultimate worship would be somehow facilitated by God himself. God would fit and sanctify our worship somehow. God would fit us to worship, and he would do so meeting the qualifications himself: he would provide the pure heart and the clean hands.

Also consider this psalm in relation to the two that came before it. Both of them are very famous. Psalm 22 is the psalm that includes the cry of dereliction that Jesus quotes on the cross, "My God, my God, why have you abandoned me?" (Ps 22:1; cf., Matt 27:46). This cry is often misunderstood when people take it to mean that somehow the Trinity was disrupted and divided at the moment of crucifixion, as if the First Person of the Trinity has abandoned the Second Person of the Trinity. This way of reading the text is theologically problematic because it imagines that the Trinity is somehow a society of different wills and emotional centers, where one divine person can be separated from another.[10] We tend to think that way most often when we have misunderstood the nature of the Son's incarnation. When Christ died on the cross, it was not the divine nature that underwent the transition from life to death. Rather, the Son died on the cross by virtue of his human nature—that is, in a nature capable of suffering—suffering for us. So why, then, would Jesus quote from this psalm? Answer: He identifies himself as the true suffering Davidic King! This cry of dereliction from the cross is a deeply profound claim to *royalty*: David's kingly suffering was a mere shadow of the substance that is Christ's.

Now, if the foregoing is the case for Christ's relation to Psalm 22, what about Psalm 23? In Psalm 22, David is crying out in the dark night of his soul, when his enemies surround him. In Psalm 23, he "[walks] through the valley of the shadow of death" (v. 4 ESV), and yet, he knows that he "*shall* dwell in the house of the Lord forever" (Ps 23:6 ESV; emphasis added). If Psalm 22 points to Good Friday, what does Psalm 23 point to if not Holy Saturday, when the body of Jesus lay in the grave? "Even though I walk through the valley of the shadow of death, I will fear no evil, for you are with me; your rod and your staff, they comfort me" (Ps 23:4 ESV). God will not *abandon the soul* of Christ to Sheol, as Ps 16:10 says. On the cross, in other words, Jesus identifies Psalm 22 with holy week and sets into motion a Davidic drama that takes him *through the valley of*

---

[10] Such an interpretation violates God's simplicity (see chap. 3).

the shadow of death. And where does Psalm 24 leave him? *Ascending the hill of the Lord.*

We ought not, therefore, mute our ears to the glorious trinitarian music that rings out from this psalm. The Lord, who *owns* the earth and the fullness thereof, requires that those who ascend his hill to stand in his holy place have clean hands and pure hearts. And knowing our inability to have clean hands and pure hearts, he came to us to be our champion: the eternal Son of God, the Lord Jesus Christ, who was incarnate and bore our humanity—*he* is the one who has clean hands and a pure heart. Therefore, he ascends the hill of the Lord, and he is welcomed as a conquering King. Having defeated sin and Satan and death; having snatched the keys to death and Hades; having disarmed the rulers and authorities, putting them to open shame in his glorious death and resurrection by taking the record of debt with its legal demands and nailing it to the cross; having achieved the righteousness for which David longed, to be given to everyone who would receive it by faith; he ascends bodily to receive his coronation as the God-man and Davidic King over all. Who is the King of glory? *The Lord of hosts, Jesus Christ, the resurrected and ascended Savior, he is the King of glory!*

Now, returning to our question about theological methodology, we might ask what this excursus on Psalm 24 implies for our doctrine of the Trinity. We insist that holding the doctrine of inseparable operations in our minds is important not only *after* we've done the work of exegesis but also as an integral part of exegesis. Remember, stated as a rule for Bible reading, the doctrine of inseparable operations can be understood as follows: "Scripture sometimes attributes to only one divine person a perfection, action, or *name* common to all three, because of some contextual fit or analogy between the common attribute and the divine person in question. Read such passages in a way that does not compromise the Trinity's essential oneness and equality."[11] Without the doctrine of inseparable operations, we might be tempted to read this psalm in erroneous ways regarding the Trinity.

On the one hand, we might be tempted to read it as if it were teaching that Yahweh was a monopersonal entity, who descended and ascended to stand back in his own holy presence. In other words, we might be tempted to read this passage as if the *Father* descended and ascended—an interpretation that would force us into conceptualizing the incarnation as a kind of modalism, wherein the Father descends *as* the Son. On the other hand, we might be tempted to read this passage in a polytheistic way, insisting that the Yahweh who descended and ascended is different from the Yahweh in whose presence he stands at the end of the psalm.

But keeping the doctrine of inseparable operations–along with its other trinitarian corollaries–gives us proper interpretive instincts when we approach this passage. It reminds us that the persons of the Trinity are distinct in their eternal relations, a distinction that makes their missions in redemptive history so fitting (for example, the Son, not the Father nor the Spirit, becomes incarnate). Yet the Father, Son, and Spirit are one in essence; therefore, the external works of the Trinity are undivided (for example, the incarnation in its entirety—from *descent* to *ascent*—is a trinitarian work that results in praise to the glory of Yahweh). In sum, the doctrine of inseparable operations helps us to make sense of Psalm 24 in trinitarian perspective, in such a way that we feel no tension to attribute praise and glory to a specific divine person, while we also render glad praise to the Lord—Yahweh—Father, Son, and Holy Spirit.

---

[11] Jamieson and Wittman, *Biblical Reasoning*, 106; emphasis added.

For the Pastor

Last, we publish this book with a particular and compassionate eye toward pastors. We wish to bless the pastor who may find himself at the end of a deep dive into trinitarian theology, coming up with newly established convictions about what *he thinks* regarding the doctrine of the Trinity, but nevertheless wondering how to begin the rewarding but laborious process of leading his flock to the insights that have gripped his own heart. Where should he start? How should he initiate his parishioners into the ocean of "the deep things of God"? Or, to change metaphors, having climbed the steep mountain of dogmatic and historical theology to see the breathtaking vistas of classical trinitarianism, he may be wondering about the best route to take his flock on. How can he guide his flock to arrive here, without losing any of them along the way, so that they might see what he sees? We commend this book as a demonstration of what such a venture might look like. Our prayerful desire is that the Holy Trinity might not be merely affirmed by pastors and church members but rather *proclaimed from pulpits* near and far.

CHAPTER ONE

A Rediscovery
The Centrality of Trinitarian Theology

Before we can *proclaim* the doctrine of the Trinity, it must be rediscovered. What does it mean to *rediscover* the doctrine of the Trinity? What might we be after in such a venture? The word "re-discovery" implies that something has been lost—what was once acknowledged (what was previously "discovered") is now forgotten or minimized and must be "rediscovered." Is such a word warranted? After all, it would be very difficult to find a professing Christian who has never even heard of the doctrine. If asked to describe this word, "Trinity," your average Christian will probably say something like, God is "one God and three Persons: Father, Son, and Holy Spirit," which is true. So, does the present state of Christianity call for the *rediscovery* of a doctrine that virtually every Christian affirms (at least in theory)? The answer is yes, because, while the straightforward confession that God is "one God and three Persons" is shared by virtually all professing Christians, the fact is that some Christians today annex the doctrine to a back room of their minds, where it remains, collecting dust, until they are explicitly asked about it. And in that sense, as we will show later in the chapter, the doctrine of the Trinity has been *lost*.

To illustrate, we might be so bold as to assume most Christians, if asked what the doctrine of the Trinity has to do with their Bible reading, would not be prepared to give an answer because the importance of the Trinity to their Bible reading has probably never occurred to them. Take, for example, the first two verses of Peter's first pastoral epistle: "Peter, an apostle of Jesus Christ: To those chosen, living as exiles dispersed abroad in Pontus, Galatia, Cappadocia, Asia, and Bithynia, chosen according to the foreknowledge of God the Father, through the sanctifying work of the Spirit, to be obedient and to be sprinkled with the blood of Jesus Christ"(1 Pet 1:1–2). Longtime readers of the Bible will have read these verses countless times. Yet, they likely will not have spent much time on these verses because, of course, they are simply the introductory greetings Peter gives before delving into the *purpose* of his letter. As a result, too few readers today appreciate the trinitarian shape of these words. Again, it does not even occur to most readers to ask what the introductory words of a pastoral epistle can teach us about the doctrine of the Trinity, or how the doctrine of the Trinity should inform our reading. But this has not always been the case. On this passage, the fourth-century church father, Gregory of Nyssa, wrote these words:

> We are redeemed from death, receiving the gracious gift of immortality, through faith in Father, Son, and Holy Spirit. These names teach us that we mustn't connect the Holy Trinity with the lowly nature of a servant or created thing, nor anything unworthy of the Father's splendor. From faith in the Holy Trinity comes our life, springing first from the Father, the God of all, flowing to us through

the Son, and working in us by the Holy Spirit. Having this full assurance, we are baptized as the Lord commanded, believe what we are baptized into, and maintain what we believe. Thus our baptism, faith, and praise, are to Father, Son, and Holy Spirit.[1]

What we have said here about the Trinity and Bible reading would be true if the average Christian were asked about the Trinity's relevance for his evangelism, or prayer life, or worship, or his experience of coming to faith, or his experience of sanctification over the course of his earthly pilgrimage, or his hope for heaven, and so on. The plain truth is that he probably hasn't thought about what the confession of God's triune nature has to do with any of these things. But notice that these topics concern the very basics of the Christian life. If the doctrine of the Trinity does not speak to these topics, it does not speak to *the Christian life*. Surely that conclusion is not an option for us.

This book is an invitation for Christians to rediscover the centrality of God in the Christian life. We want readers not merely to affirm God's triune life, but to *delight* in the triune God! Our contention is that recovering the biblical and historic doctrine of the Holy Trinity, and giving it the central and privileged place in *all* our thinking, will only enrich our lives. There is more joy to be had by working to reconceptualize the Christian life and Christian theology with the Trinity at the gravitational center—holding *all* other things in their proper place in relation to *Father, Son, and Spirit*.

With this promise also comes a sober warning, however. This will not be *easy*. Indeed, the doctrine of the Trinity *should not* be easy— we are talking about God, who is necessarily incomprehensible to

---

[1] Gregory of Nyssa, Letter 2, "To the City of Sebasteia."

limited creatures like us. If he were not—if knowledge of this God were circumscribable to our thoughtlife—we would not be dealing with God, but rather with an idol.

What does this mean? It means that we may stretch you over the course of these chapters. In this book we will introduce language that is probably *unfamiliar* for most of us. We will focus a lot on precision of speech and grammar. We will focus on how we *should* and how we *should not* talk about God, and at some points it may seem like we are splitting hairs or being overly fastidious with our use of words. But if you hang in there, we promise you the payoff is worth it!

Since this pilgrimage will require us to climb some high mountains, we will need the help of the greatest trinitarian theologians of the past. They have travelled this terrain before us and are trustworthy guides. To that end, we will listen to the saints within the great tradition of the Christian faith as they wrestled over the course of the past two thousand years with the very same questions that occupy this book. And we will do this *eagerly*. Gratitude for where God has placed us in history should compel us to receive our Christian heritage from the past not reluctantly or begrudgingly, but with a heart of thanksgiving.

In other words, we should read our Bibles not only *in the church* but also *with the church*—and not simply with the Christians around us (as nonnegotiable and crucial as that is) but also with Christians who have gone before us. Jesus Christ promised us in Matt 16:18, "I will build my church, and the gates of Hades will not overpower it." When we read the Word of God with the people of God—including the people of God from the past—we bank on Christ's promise that he would build his church and that the gates of hell would not prevail against it. The sad reality is that many of us today do not even realize what a treasure we have in our ecclesial family heritage.

Imagine, for example, growing up in a very poor house, isolated from any signs of joy, with little food or friends or entertainment or leisure or anything to shape your imagination beyond the tiny confines of your isolated home. And then imagine discovering that less than a mile down the road, you have wealthy and generous relatives who would love for nothing more than to have you over to play with your cousins, swim in their pool, and eat the kind of food of which you had only heard rumors. Not only that, but in meeting these wealthy and generous relatives, you are introduced to an entire family lineage—all with a heritage that belongs to *you*. With shock, you discover that you had lived so much of your life needlessly impoverished, ignorantly estranged from the best family you could ask for! Many of us Christians today find ourselves in a similar situation: we are cut off and estranged from a family lineage without even knowing better. In the history of Christianity's great tradition, there is a rich heritage that rightly belongs to us. It is a living tradition that we are invited to participate in *as* we wrestle with the doctrine of the Trinity.

The Need for Our Rediscovery

Question: Why must we center all of Christian theology and practice on the Trinity? Answer: Because the God whom we worship *is triune*. We cannot worship God rightly until we come to know him truly. This means—and we say this without a hint of exaggeration—sound trinitarian theology is necessary for us to fulfill our chief end as human beings. Consider the Westminster Larger Catechism's first question and answer:

> Q. What is the chief and highest end of man?
> A. Man's chief and highest end is to glorify God, and fully to enjoy him for ever.[2]

God made us for himself. To the degree that glorifying and enjoying God truly is our chief end, trinitarian theology is necessary. How can one glorify God and how can one enjoy God without *getting to know him*? Who is this God whom we are to glorify? Why ought this God be enjoyed? *We cannot answer these questions without theology.*

The importance of objective truth is worth stressing here. "Good intentions" simply are not sufficient on this matter. A Muslim may genuinely want to glorify God when he bows down toward Mecca five times a day, but he does not glorify God by his genuineness. He is genuinely wrong about who God is, and so he is prevented from living out his chief end. Theology makes the difference between glorifying God and glorifying an idol.

Consider the striking example of Lev 10:1–7. Aaron—the high priest of Israel—and all of the Levitical priests were instructed by Yahweh, at the mouth of Moses, on how they were to worship him. In Leviticus 9, Aaron obeys the instructions of Moses, and Yahweh vindicates his faithfulness by responding in power: "Fire came from the Lord and consumed the burnt offering and the fat portions on the altar. And when all the people saw it, they shouted and fell facedown" (Lev 9:24). But in the very next chapter, Aaron's faithful worship is sharply contrasted with the faithless worship of his two sons: Nadab and Abihu. Rather than following the clear example laid out by their father in the previous chapter, Nadab and Abihu disregarded Yahweh's instructions. Apparently, they assumed that

---

[2] Westminster Larger Catechism, Q. 1 (1647) (public domain).

Yahweh did not care about *how* he was worshipped, and so, in a spirit of innovation and (possibly) good intentions, they "presented unauthorized fire before the Lord, which he had not commanded them to do" (Lev 10:1). In response to this, Yahweh sent fire and "consumed them, and they died before the Lord" (Lev 10:2). Evidently, God cares about *how* we worship him. And how we worship him depends entirely on who we think he is.

However, we are not merely forced to read between the lines of a narrative like Leviticus 10—as clear as it is—since God himself confirms as much *directly*. Consider these words he spoke through the prophet Jeremiah:

> This is what the Lord says:
> The wise person should not boast in his wisdom;
> the strong should not boast in his strength;
> the wealthy should not boast in his wealth.
> But the one who boasts should boast in this:
> that he understands and knows me—
> that I am the Lord, showing faithful love,
> justice, and righteousness on the earth,
> for I delight in these things.
> This is the Lord's declaration. (Jer 9:23–24)

The doctrine of the Trinity is central to Christianity because it gets at *who God is*. If we get the Trinity wrong, everything else goes wrong. There is, in fact, no gospel—the central message of "good news" that defines the Christian community—without the doctrine of Trinity. It is not possible for our trinitarian theology to go wrong without such an error perverting our understanding of the gospel. The stakes are *that* high.

If you do not believe us, simply call your attention to the sobering results of the recent Ligonier Ministries 2020 State of Theology report.[3] Of the 3,002 participants who took this survey, 65 percent (approximately two-thirds) of those who identified as evangelical agreed with the statement, "Jesus is the first and greatest being *created by God*." But friends, that statement is *not* orthodox Christianity. Such a statement more closely resembles the ancient heresy of Arianism, which propagates a false gospel. A Jesus who is "the first and greatest being created by God" is not the Jesus of the Bible or the historic Christian faith, and such a Jesus cannot save. But not a few professing evangelical Christians testify that this Jesus is the Jesus they confess to believe in. This means the rediscovery of trinitarian doctrine is *painfully* necessary. So, if we get the Trinity wrong, everything goes wrong; and if we get it right, we are well on our way to living out our chief end as human beings.

To clarify, our central claim of the Trinity's importance to all Christian theology and practice does *not* mean that the Christian who has a beginner's understanding of the Trinity is a false believer. But it does mean that you *cannot* be a Christian if you *deny* the doctrine of the Trinity. A "non-trinitarian Christian" is an oxymoron—a contradiction of terms. Further, all of this implies that Christians who have little knowledge of the Trinity should—if their appetites are healthy—aspire to *grow* in the grace and knowledge of our triune God. While you may not be required to have a robust understanding of the Trinity as a Christian, if you are a Christian, you *will* want to increase in your understanding. As Christians, we should strive for our meditations on God to be more and more honoring to him and therefore more and more accurate. All this

---

[3] "The State of American Theology Study 2020," commissioned by Ligonier Ministries, Lifeway Research, 9, 48; emphasis added; https://research.lifeway.com/wp-content/uploads/2020/09/Ligonier-State-of-Theology-2020-Report.pdf.

should matter to us, and it should matter to us as an evidence of our love for God. This is Paul's point in Colossians 1:

> For this reason also, since the day we heard this, we haven't stopped praying for you. We are asking that you may be filled with the knowledge of his will in all wisdom and spiritual understanding, so that you may walk worthy of the Lord, fully pleasing to him: bearing fruit in every good work and growing in the knowledge of God, being strengthened with all power, according to his glorious might, so that you may have great endurance and patience, joyfully giving thanks to the Father, who has enabled you to share in the saints' inheritance in the light. (vv. 9–12)

Here, Paul tells the Colossians that he prays for them to be "filled with the knowledge of his will in all wisdom and spiritual understanding," and he therefore is not embarrassed in the slightest to commend *thinking*. He wants the Colossians to grow in their knowledge of God, even as he also wants them to "walk worthy of the Lord, fully pleasing to him: bearing fruit." But Paul does not see these two activities (*thinking* and *walking*, increasing in knowledge and faithful obedience) as two distinct answers to two distinct prayers. Rather, the *way* the Colossians will "walk worthy of the Lord, fully pleasing to him" is *by* "growing in the knowledge of God," which is why he joins these two phrases with "*so that you may.*" He wants them to increase in knowledge *so as to walk* in a manner wherein they will bear fruit, one fruit of which is the increase of more knowledge (v. 10), which will beget more fruit bearing, which will beget more knowledge, and so on. Right knowledge produces right living before God; right living before God produces godly fruit; godly fruit includes right knowledge; and around we go.

The Ethos of Our Rediscovery

If our investigation of trinitarian theology comes from a deep desire to know and love God better, then our rediscovery will be shaped by a particular ethos. Our meditations on the Trinity are to be (1) instructional, (2) humble, and (3) worshipful. By "instructional," we intend to emphasize what the early Christians called *catechesis*. This was the process whereby a new believer (the catechumen) was initiated (via baptism) into the Christian family and was *prepared* for this initiation through instruction (catechesis). Much of the catechesis process involves questions and answers. (This is what a catechism is—a collection of instructional questions and answers.) Instruction, for the catechumens, happened by *recitation*. In this way, this book will be catechetical: it will repeatedly raise questions and answer them. And the truths that we shall "recite together" in this book are truths that have been held and taught and proclaimed throughout the history of the Christian church. We shall recite words and concepts and categories that virtually every Christian generation—until the modern era—has considered important. Indeed, these are truths that the great tradition fought hard to maintain and pass down to us. To put the matter plainly, we affirm that the trinitarian theology we receive and impart in this book is part of the deposit of faith handed down to us from generation to generation; it is an essential part of the "faith that was delivered to the saints once for all" (Jude v. 3). And this means we should receive these with *humility*.

Our humility here has a twofold justification. First, as has already been said, the incomprehensibility of God *demands* humility. What do we have that we did not receive (cf., 1 Cor 4:7)? What we concern ourselves with here are deep mysteries beyond the comprehension of any creature. The fact that a book like this exists at all is a testimony to God's incredible grace. Unless he were to reveal himself as triune through his mighty acts and missions in human history and his inspired Word, we would not have a doctrine of the Trinity of which to speak. We would have nothing to *say*. While God's triune nature would be no less *real* than it is, *we* would be none the wiser. Therefore, we approach this doctrine as beggars: on our knees, heads bowed and palms up. We *receive*.

Second, our humility on this doctrine is demanded because it is particularly lacking in our present age. We suffer from a deadly ailment C. S. Lewis dubbed "chronological snobbery."[4] This is the tendency to think that *recent* or *contemporary* or *new* amounts to *better*. If our age is anything at all, it is chronologically snobbish—eager to sit in the place of judgment over the past and cancel anyone and everyone it deems unworthy. Our age, as a chronologically snobbish age, is profoundly ungrateful, and we have a moral and spiritual duty to be countercultural in this respect. We should reject the tendency that says, "All that stuff about theology and philosophy does not matter; let's just worship Jesus and keep it simple."

We mention this intellectual ailment here because Christians in the modern era are not used to talking about God the way Christians of the past talked about God, and as a result, we may be tempted to avoid the difficult work of understanding our heritage. But we should be slow to dismiss our forefathers simply because there is a learning curve for us to think about God the way that they did. We may be tempted to assume that their theological

---

[4] C. S. Lewis, *Surprised by Joy: The Shape of My Early Life* (New York: Harcourt Brace, 1955), 201.

concerns were excessively tedious and overly speculative and therefore unnecessary. We should be hesitant to assume that we know better than they what is essential and what is unimportant. Before we dismiss the complex and difficult concepts related to trinitarian theology, we should ask why Christians have fought so hard to preserve them for nearly two thousand years. Might they have had good reasons for doing so? If we ask that question with all sincerity and labor to understand our theological forefathers in their context, grasping the concerns that occupied their attention, we believe we will come to agree with those Christians on the importance of their theological system. We will come to agree with them because we shall see that nothing less than *worship* is on the line.

This, in case you were wondering, is the "usefulness" of a book like this. In our pragmatic age, we are used to demanding the practicality of things. "If it cannot be put into immediate practical use," we say, "I do not want to hear it." By contrast, what we wish to commend to you is the value of theological contemplation not as a means to an end but as an end itself. Sometimes the only charge left (the only "practical application" of a doctrine) is to *behold your God*—to adore him, to let yourself and your petty problems be forgotten and dwarfed by God's glorious grandeur, to be gripped as Jonathan Edwards was when he read 1 Tim 1:17. Recounting the experience, Edwards wrote:

> As I read the words, there came into my soul, and was as it were diffused through it, a sense of the glory of the divine being; a new sense, quite different from any thing I ever experienced before. Never any words of Scripture seemed to me as these words did. I thought with myself, how excellent a Being that was, and how happy I should

be, if I might enjoy that God, and be wrapt up to God in heaven, and be as it were swallowed up in him.[5]

Let us learn to embrace the contemplative life together. Let us give our attention unreservedly to God and his nature. If we do this, we shall certainly receive ample "devotional" and "practical" benefits from it, but this is not why we ought to give ourselves to this sacred task of theological contemplation. We ought to render our unreserved attention to God *because he is worthy of nothing less*. What is worth our attention more than this? Let us learn to truly say, with David, "One thing have I asked of the Lord, that will I seek after: that I may dwell in the house of the Lord all the days of my life, to gaze upon the beauty of the Lord and to inquire in his temple" (Ps 27:4 ESV). Again, our older brother C. S. Lewis speaks to us with the wisdom of experience on this matter:

> For my own part, I tend to find the doctrinal books often more helpful in devotion than the devotional books, and I rather suspect that the same experience may await many others. I believe that many who find that "nothing happens" when they sit down, or kneel down, to a book of devotion, would find that the heart sings unbidden while they are working their way through a tough bit of theology with a pipe in their teeth and a pencil in their hand.[6]

---

[5] Jonathan Edwards (1716), *Works of Jonathan Edwards Online,* vol. 16, *Letters and Personal Writings,* ed. George S. Claghorn, 792.

[6] C. S. Lewis, "On the Reading of Old Books." *God in the Dock: Essays on Theology and Ethics,* ed. Walter Hooper (Grand Rapids: Eerdmans, 1970), 205.

With these introductory remarks out of the way, let us turn our attention to the fourth century to learn from our older brothers of the faith.

Fourth-Century Worship Wars

Today, it is not uncommon for new congregational worship songs to make it into the catalogues of local church song lists. Despite the unique favorite songs that vary from church to church, evangelicals who travel across the United States are likely to hear familiar lyrics at like-minded local churches. Not only will they hear hymns that have become more or less timeless, which were once new songs themselves (songs like "A Mighty Fortress Is Our God" and "It Is Well with My Soul"), they are also likely to hear well-worn songs that have been written in the past few decades (songs like "In Christ Alone" and "How Great is Our God"). This sharing of doxological scripts has always been the case for the church. In fact, many scholars believe some of our most cherished New Testament passages are actually lyrics from early Christian hymns that had made their way, organically, into the vocabulary of the church (e.g., Col 1:15–18; Phil 2:5–11). This was also not uncommon in the early centuries following the New Testament. In fact, if you could travel back in time to the second decade of the fourth century, and if you could make your way into a local church service in Alexandria—one of the greatest cities in the Roman Empire—you would likely hear a song that crescendos into a pithy line, "There was a time when the Son was not." After inquiring, you would discover that this song was written by one of the day's "celebrity pastors" by the name of Arius (250–336) and that it represents no small controversy in the region.

Arius taught that the Son, though highly exalted and instrumental in the creation of all else, is the first of the Father's creation. According to Arius, the doctrine of divine simplicity (see chapter 3 for more on this doctrine) means that the Son *must* be ontologically distinct from the Father. For if God is one, and if God's oneness tolerates no *parts,* how can we say that the Son is God? Would we not then have to argue that God is *part* Father and *part* Son and therefore not simple? And besides, doesn't the Scripture itself teach that the Son was the *firstborn* of the Father's creation (Col 1:15), and is he not the Word—the Wisdom—who was "acquired" and "formed" at "the beginning" of creation (cf., Prov 8:22–24; John 1:1–3)? So, reasoned Arius, while we can speak highly of the Son, and even refer to him as a kind of "god" through whom the rest of creation was made, we must not delude ourselves into believing contradictions. The Son is the first and greatest being of the Father's creation but still sits squarely on that *creature* side of the Creator-creature divide. Therefore, we can still talk about the Father and Son being *one* and *unified* in a sense. But their unity, according to Arius and his followers, was not a unity of *essence,* but rather a unity—or harmony—of wills. In fact, the Son, whose will is distinct from the Father's in Arius's system, is himself the *product* of the Father's will.

Arius's most prominent critic was the bishop of Alexandria named, interestingly enough, Alexander (250–326). Alexander vehemently opposed Arius and insisted that the Father and Son were of the same essence (*homoousios*). Alexander's most famous pupil was an African pastor named Athanasius (ca. 293–373), who took up the mantle of criticizing Arianism (i.e., Arius's teaching) with unparalleled adeptness. The controversy became so heated that it eventuated in the Council of Nicaea, where many pastors and theologians throughout the Roman Empire were summoned by Emperor Constantine to come to the city of Nicaea to work out the issue over the course of several months.[7]

The result of this council was the Nicene Creed of 325, which pronounced the shared divine essence of the Father and Son and denounced Arius and his teaching. Since Arius and his followers did not go away, the need for more precision became necessary over the course of the next few decades as the controversy continued. So, in 381 another council was held in the city of Constantinople, where the Nicene Creed of 325 was expanded and clarified. This creed is sometimes referred to as the Nicene-Constantinopolitan Creed or the Constantinopolitan Creed, but most often it is simply referred to as the Nicene Creed (which, we believe, is appropriate, since it is a *natural* and *essential* expansion of the original Nicene Creed).

These councils and their respective creeds did not automatically convince the undecided Christian in the fourth century, nor did they silence the opposition. For this reason, a legacy of pro-Nicene defenders quickly developed in the subsequent decades and centuries. As mentioned before, chief among these defenders was Alexander's protégé, Athanasius. Importantly, Athanasius did not marshal different proof texts than his opponents (e.g., Col 1:15; Prov 8:22–24), nor did he appeal to different philosophical ideas (e.g., the doctrine of divine simplicity). He differed, rather, in his hermeneutical and exegetical decisions. Rather than shrinking

---

[7] This historical survey is intentionally brief. For a thorough telling of the events and thought that led up to Nicaea, see Lewis Ayers, *Nicaea and Its Legacy: An Approach to Fourth-Century Trinitarian Theology* (New York: Oxford University Press, 2009); Khaled Anatolios, *Retrieving Nicaea: The Development and Meaning of Trinitarian Doctrine* (Grand Rapids: Baker Academic, 2018); and R. P. C. Hansen, *The Search for the Christian God: The Arian Controversy* (Grand Rapids: Baker Academic, 2005).

back from doctrines like divine simplicity, Athanasius defended the Son's divinity *on the grounds* of divine simplicity. For example, Athanasius wrote:

> Who will presume to say that the radiance is unlike and foreign to the sun? rather who, thus considering the radiance relatively to the sun, and the identity of the light, would not say with confidence, "Truly the light and the radiance are one, and the one is manifested in the other, and the radiance is in the sun, so that whoso sees this, sees that also?" but such a oneness and natural property, what should it be named by those who believe and see aright but Offspring one in essence? and God's Offspring what should we fittingly and suitably consider, but Word, and Wisdom, and Power? Which it were a sin to say was foreign to the Father, or a crime even to imagine as other than with Him everlastingly.[8]

For Athanasius, along with the rest of the pro-Nicene fathers, the persons of the Trinity are not *parts* of the divine nature. If they were, the doctrine of divine simplicity *would* make trinitarian theology incoherent and self-contradictory. Instead, he understood the Father, Son, and Spirit as personal subsistences of the one, simple, divine nature.

Likewise, the pro-Nicene fathers used the same Scripture passages the Arians used. However, whereas the Arians used those passages to *undermine* the Son's divinity, the pro-Nicene fathers used them to *prove* the Son's divinity. How did they do this? The fact is, their hermeneutic was far more careful and far more

---

[8] Athanasius, *De Decretis*, 5.24. Original capitalization preserved. See also, *Against the Arians*, 27.36.

sophisticated than that of their opponents, who failed to reason along the lines of Scripture's logic and instead crudely appealed to surface-level interpretations to bolster up their own agendas.[9] The pro-Nicene fathers, by contrast, were careful to distinguish between *theologia* and *oikonomia*—"theology" and "economy," or, *who God is in himself* and *how God reveals himself in his acts* (for more on this distinction, see chapter 2). The Father "[giving] birth" to Wisdom "before the mountains were established" (Prov 8:25) does not bespeak the Father *creating* his own wisdom as an exercise of will *chronologically* before the rest of creation.[10] Such an interpretation

---

[9] They did this, we might add, in such a way that their conclusion of one text, like Prov 8:22, contradicted the indisputable meanings of others, like John 10:30. If Proverbs 8 reveals that the Son is a creature, why then would Jesus claim to be one with the Father? Again, anti-Nicene figures might argue that Jesus's oneness with the Father is a unity of purpose—the Father and the Son are "on the same page." But such an explanation does not make sense of the Jews' response to attempt to kill Jesus. Apparently, *they* believed Jesus was making himself out to be God and considered his words blasphemous (John 10:33). For his own part, Jesus did not insist they had misunderstood him but confirmed their interpretation of his words, which, of course, contradicts the Arian interpretation of Prov 8:22. For more on John 10 and this interaction between Jesus and the Jews, see chapter 5.

[10] For example, Matthew Y. Emerson summarizes, "For Proverbs 8:22 and 25, therefore, the pro-Nicene theologians read a proverbial text, connected closely to New Testament Wisdom Christology passages, that speaks of 'begot' and 'created' as referring to two different periods in the economy of salvation: verse 22 refers to the incarnation (especially for Athanasius) while verse 25 refers to the eternal Logos. This latter point led them to attempt to clearly articulate how divine Wisdom, as the Second Person of the Trinity, could be 'begotten' of the Father while also being eternally and equally God. For the early Christian theologians, eternal generation is the answer to this question. Further, it is a thoroughly textual answer, grounded in clear hermeneutical methods and theological commitments." Matthew Y. Emmerson, "The Role of Proverbs 8: Eternal

implies that there was a time when the Father did not have wisdom and, further, that the Father requires creation for the exercise of his own wisdom (an implication which would pose a problem for the doctrines of God's simplicity and his *aseity*—his self-sufficiency). Rather, this description is a poetic description of God's infinite Wisdom and the Son's timelessly eternal relation of origin to the Father—never was the Father without his Wisdom—even "before the mountains were established."[11]

Again, we must keep in mind that the debates in the fourth century were not about whether the Father and Son (and Spirit) were united. Almost everyone agreed that they were. The debate was surrounding whether their unity was a unity of *will* or a unity of *being*. If the former, then the Son is a product of the Father's will and therefore subordinate. If the latter, then the Son is one with the Father, as Jesus says in John 10:30, and therefore equal in power and glory. The heterodox answer is that they are merely united in their will—they are *working* together—but the orthodox answer is that they are united in their being—they share the same divine essence.[12]

As mentioned before, the practical issue really comes down to worship: Is it fitting to worship Jesus in any sense? If he is a creature, the answer is unambiguously *no*. This was one of Athanasius's primary criticisms of Arius, who was involved in *Christian* worship—if Arius's doctrine was right, Christian worship of Jesus, the Word, is

---

Generation and Hermeneutics Ancient and Modern," in Fred Sanders and Scott R. Swain, eds., *Retrieving Eternal Generation* (Grand Rapids: Zondervan Academic, 2017), 54.

[11] For similar, contemporary, renderings of this passage, see Jason S. DeRouchie's and Craig A. Carter's respective chapters in Brian J. Tabb and Andrew M. King, eds., *Five Views of Christ in the Old Testament* (Grand Rapids: Zondervan Academic, 2022).

[12] See Anatolios, *Retrieving Nicaea*, 42–98.

altogether unfitting and blasphemous. If Arius was right, in other words, the Jews acted righteously by picking up stones to execute Jesus on the grounds of blasphemy. Therefore, the Nicene Creed was not merely concerned with establishing boundaries for orthodoxy. The creed also functions as a form of discipleship and instruction: it provides proper grammar for how to talk about the Trinity for the sake of *right worship*.

The Nicene Creed: Our Theological Heritage

So, what *does* the Nicene Creed teach us about our doxological speech? Let us consider it briefly. The creed is divided up into three main sections, each under the heading of a divine person: the Father, the Son, and the Holy Spirit. Let us call our attention first to the initial statements made about God at the beginning of each section in the creed:[13]

> I believe in *one God*, the Father Almighty,
>> Maker of heaven and earth, and of all things visible and invisible.
>
> And in *one Lord Jesus Christ*, the only-begotten Son of God,
>> begotten of the Father before all worlds;
>> God of God, Light of Light, very God of very God;
>> begotten, not made, being of one substance with the Father,
>> by whom all things were made. . . .
>
> And I believe in the Holy Spirit, *the Lord and Giver of life*;

---

[13] Chad Van Dixhoorn, *Creeds, Confessions, and Catechisms: A Reader's Edition* (Wheaton, IL: Crossway, 2022), 17–18; emphasis added.

who proceeds from the Father and the Son;
who with the Father and the Son together is worshiped and glorified.

So, what does the creed teach us about the Trinity? First, it affirms that there is "one God . . . one Lord . . . [and one] Giver of life"—it affirms, in other words, the unity and singularity of God. There is one God and one God *only*. This statement affirms that there is one divine nature—one divine essence—which is undivided and eternal.

The divine nature is simple, meaning it cannot be divided into parts or passions. All that is in God *is* God. God does not simply *have* goodness or love or holiness, for example; he *is* absolute goodness, and his goodness *is* absolute love and holiness. What we experience when we encounter God's love is not different from his holiness. God's love for us is God's "God-ness" freely given. Conversely, what unbelievers experience when they experience God's wrath in hell is not different from his goodness or holiness: God's wrath toward sinners is an expression of God's holiness—his "God-ness" manifested in light of human sin. (This is why *holiness*, not *wrath*, is rightly identified as an attribute of God. We need sin to understand wrath, which means wrath cannot be a divine attribute. Rather, wrath is what holiness looks like when sin is in view.) God is eternally himself. He does not change; we do. This is what we mean when we talk of God's *simple, divine nature*. This God does not owe his existence to another. His timelessly eternal perfection means that he could not have anything added or diminished, increased or decreased—his perfection means that he is himself from age to age. His essence is *one*. "Listen, Israel: The Lord our God, the Lord is one" (Deut 6:4).

And yet, this undivided divine essence exists eternally in what we call *three distinct modes of subsistence*. There are three names, three persons, three *relations*, which are at various points throughout the Scriptures identified with this one undivided essence. For example, in 1 Cor 8:6, Paul refers to this declaration of God's unity from Deut 6:4 ("The LORD our God, the LORD is one"), but astonishingly he implicates Jesus in that divine unity as well. Paul says, "For us there is one God, the Father. All things are from him, and we exist for him." Now, this language is not all that astonishing, and it seems pretty clear that Paul intends for our minds to think back on Deut 6:4. But then he goes on to say, "*And there is one Lord*, Jesus Christ. *All things are through him, and we exist through him*" (1 Cor 8:6; emphasis added).

This is not an accidental afterthought. Do not miss the gravity of what Paul does with this verse. By including the Lord Jesus with this language of "One," Paul intends for his readers to *forever* think back on Israel's axiomatic, monotheistic confession (i.e., Deut 6:4) with *Christ* in view, included in that confession. According to Paul, all things are *from the Father* and *through the Son*. This is how he understands the monotheistic confession of Yahweh's *oneness*, and this is how he intends for us to understand it as well. So in light of passages like this, the Nicene Creed affirms that the Son is "begotten of the Father before all worlds; God of God, Light of Light, very God of very God; begotten, not made, being of one substance [or *essence* or *nature*] with the Father." And the Holy Spirit, the creed affirms, "proceeds from the Father and the Son; who with the Father and the Son together is worshiped and glorified." So this one, undivided, singular divine nature eternally exists *as* the Father begetting the Son and the Spirit proceeding from the Father and the Son. For God to be

God is for the Father to beget the Son, and the Father and Son to spirate the Spirit.[14]

Now, what exactly does this term *beget* mean? We do not use that word *beget* very often, but it communicates something important about the divine nature the Father and Son share. We know that human fathers beget human sons. They do not beget, for example, dogs. Nor do earthly people *make* sons in the same way that they may *make* a painting or a sculpture. Such a work of art may *resemble* a man, but it does not render the artist a father; the only thing that does that is his begetting of *children*. Like begets like. Nature begets nature. Similarly, what God *begets* is God—the Father's nature is divine, so the Son he *begets* is also divine. As the church fathers liked to say, the Son is begotten from the Father's divine nature.[15] But unlike the reality of human fathers begetting human sons, this divine begetting by the Father of the Son has no beginning and no end. The Son's is an *eternal* "begottenness." There is no "before" the Father begot the Son. This "begetting" is *timeless*. "God of God, Light of Light, very God of very God; begotten, not made."[16]

What the creed affirms, then, is that between the chasm of the Creator and the creature—between the eternal Maker and the finite

---

[14] The tautological awkwardness of this word "spirate" helps illustrate the limitation of our words. The Spirit's procession from the Father and the Son is distinct from the Son's procession of eternal generation from the Father alone. Saying that the Spirit is spirated is to note the Third Person's procession from the Father and the Son in which the Father and Son breathe out, or spirate, the Spirit.

[15] For examples from the church fathers to the Reformed Orthodox, see Barrett, *Simply Trinity*, especially chapters 2 and 6.

[16] See more on the nature of eternal generation in chapter 4.

made—there is *one Being*, one *essence*, one *nature* on the Creator side. Father, Son, and Spirit eternally subsist in one divine nature. They are, in the words of the creed itself, *consubstantial* with one another. "To say that Father, Son, and Spirit are consubstantial," D. Glenn Butner Jr. notes, "is to affirm that each has what is necessary to count as fully and equally divine."[17]

You are not asked, friends, to *comprehend this*. You are asked, rather, to confess it and revel in it. This is why we should regularly confess the Nicene Creed together. In doing so, we self-consciously join our witness with the historic Christian church that Christ began to build in the first century, that he continued to build in the fourth century when the Nicene Creed was written, and that he has continued to build throughout the centuries as his people have confessed their allegiance to the one God over all—the Father, Son, and Holy Spirit.

Poetry in Service of Praise

We might be helped in getting at the difference between *comprehending* this truth and *reveling* in it with the aid of poetry. There is something about poetry that allows one to tap into the deep undercurrents of reality. If "the heavens declare the glory of God, and the expanse proclaims the work of his hands" (Ps 19:1), and if "the heavens were made by the word of the Lord, and all the stars, by the breath of his mouth" (Ps 33:6), then divine poetry holds the world together. All creaturely existence *is* divine poetry. Fitting, then, is John's description, "All things were created through [the *Word*]" (John 1:3; emphasis added), by whom, according to

---

[17] D. Glenn Butner Jr., *Trinitarian Dogmatics: Exploring the Grammar of the Christian Doctrine of God* (Grand Rapids: Baker Academic, 2022), 43.

Paul, "all things *hold together*" (Col. 1:17; emphasis added). If you imagine that the bottom of reality is *poetry* and *music*, rather than simply taking it for granted as *there*, your understanding of your place in the world takes on an entirely different mood. This is why we should go out of our way, in the spirit of C.S. Lewis, to teach our kids that magic is *real*. What else could we call a tree's ability to take water, air, and sunlight and turn it all into apples? You can call it photosynthesis if you would like, and I like the word well enough, but children will also tell you this thing's "Christian name": *it is God's magic*.

This is why describing what happens when words come together to communicate truth, goodness, and beauty with the word *magic* is not an exaggeration. There is a deep, metaphysical correspondence between language and all of reality, and as we said before, poetry is a way of tapping into that correspondence at an incomprehensibly deep level. One of the best "word-wizards" was George Herbert, and one of the best of his "spells" is a poem called "Ungratefulness."

What kind of a spell does Herbert weave with this poem? It is a spell that simultaneously frees us from the enchantment of a sinful and bored malaise when considering the doctrines of the Trinity and the incarnation, and disabuses us of the curse of hubris regarding these profound mysteries. This is precisely how we can be sure that his spell is the good kind—the kind that taps into true *reality*. The Trinity and the incarnation are mysteries that cannot be explained away, but only *adored*, which means any articulation of these realities that does not simultaneously *enlighten* us to their grandeur and *enshroud* God in the glory cloud of inapproachable and incomprehensible light, falls short. To know God rightly is to live in the beatific place between God's mystery and revelation. Praise springs up right there, in that sweet spot. And Herbert's poem does this, for us at least, in three stanzas in the middle of the poem.[18] Here's the first:

> Thou hast but two rare Cabinets full of treasure,
> > The *Trinity* and *Incarnation*.
> Thou hast unlock'd them both,
> > And made them jewels to betroth
> > The work of thy creation
> Unto thyself in everlasting pleasure.

Here, Herbert describes the doctrines of the Trinity and the incarnation as cabinets full of treasure. Think of a chest, so full of jewels and riches that light seems to emanate off the surface once opened. And Herbert (rightly) praises God for the fact that both of these treasure chests have been unlocked and opened by God, for his glory and good pleasure. He then goes on to describe each of these "chests" respectively.

> The statelier Cabinet is the *Trinity*,
> > Whose sparkling light access denies
> > > Therefore thou dost not show
> > This fully to us, till death blow
> > > The dust into our eyes;
> > For by that powder thou wilt make us see.

The cabinet labeled "Trinity" is, according to Herbert, the "statelier" of the two. It's so august and its light so intense that we can't even look at it. "Access" he says, is "denie[d]." And yet, the cabinet is

---

[18] The Herbert quotations that follow are from "Ungratefulness," in *The Works of George Herbert*, 2nd ed., vol. 2, *The Temple: Sacred Poems and Private Ejaculations* (London: Pickering, 1838), 79–80; emphasis added.

opened, and we see that light is coming from it. God truly has revealed his triune nature. But he has not done this "fully." Will he ever? Yes, Herbert says, but first our eyes need to be adjusted. First, death has to blow its dust into our eyes so that by its powder we can see. Aren't those paradoxes simply delightful? The language Herbert uses is surprising in exactly the way it should be if we are talking about a doctrine as mysterious and grand as the Trinity. For the Christian, the dust that death blows in our eyes does not obscure our vision, it *clears* it! No longer will the cataracts of sin obscure the glory of the Trinity, once in death we are given powder for our eyes to see rightly—that is, in the beatific vision. In the meantime, God has been gracious to give us another cabinet, whose treasures are imminently *accessible* to us.

> But all thy sweets are pack'd up in the other;
> > Thy mercies thither flock and flow:
> > > That, as the first affrights,
> > > This may allure us with delights:
> > > > Because this box we know;
> > For we have all of us just such another.

Here, in this cabinet labeled "Incarnation," all God's "sweets are packed up." In Christ, we have all the treasures of heaven, and they are accessible to us precisely because he was made *like us*. The Word became flesh and tabernacled among us (John 1:14). Therefore, where the Trinity "affrights"—where it intimidates us and causes us to shield our eyes in godly fear—the incarnation "allure[s] us with delights." We are allured by the delights found in Christ, and our desire is often awakened by spells like this one from Herbert. This is what we may call "good magic." It taps into the reality of the cosmos and is therefore poetry in service of praise.

Implications for the Christian Life

In closing, we offer a few pastoral reflections and exhortations for the enrichment of your Christian life. The first exhortation is to *continue to press into this doctrine for the sake of worship*. Do not mentally check out of this book's subject matter! Be willing to be stretched. Be willing to be challenged. Be willing to have your view of God grow and develop and—in some cases—be corrected. Press in and contend yourself not only to love the Lord your God with all your heart, but also with all your *soul* and *strength* (Deut 6:5). The God who saves you in the gospel is triune, and appreciating the gospel—worshipping the God of the gospel—means confessing his triune nature. The God who saved you, believer, is the eternal Father, who in the "fullness of time" sent the eternal Son in temporal, finite flesh, to purchase your freedom from sin with his own blood, to unite you to himself by the powerful working of the eternal Holy Spirit, so as to swallow you up into the eternal fire of triune Love and Life (Gal 4:4 ESV)! Is he not worthy of the first fruits of your worshipful attention?

To return to the introduction of this chapter, we have already seen how the basic Christian understanding of the Trinity, which can be summarized in the well-known formula "one God in three persons," is rather minimalistic. While this is of course a *true* statement, it does not do justice to how rich the biblical doctrine of the Trinity really is. The worry with overly simplistic formulations, though they have their place, is that they can fail to explain the scriptural meaning. This doctrine—the *real* Trinity, the biblical and creedal and *catholic* Trinity—is hard mental work. But like most good things that require hard work, what you gain by putting in the patient work is well worth the effort.

Second, remember that you are *already* caught up in this triune life. The Trinity has swept you up into the eternal love of the Father,

Son, and Spirit, and you participate in this triune life when you pray to the Father, through the mediation of the Son, by the ministry of the Holy Spirit. You are invited, therefore, to deepen your understanding of this triune God you worship for his glory and your joy. You are invited, like Paul says in Col 1:9–10, to "be filled with the knowledge of his will in all wisdom and spiritual understanding, so that you may walk worthy of the Lord, fully pleasing to him: bearing fruit in every good work and *growing in the knowledge of God*" (emphasis added). In other words, your life—whether you see it or not—has a deeply trinitarian shape. Working toward a robust doctrine of the Trinity will only aid you in both seeing and articulating the beauty of participating in this triune life.

Now, we should simply acknowledge that the Christian life is often full of struggles and hardship. Many of you who are reading this may be going through various trials—perhaps the most difficult season of your life. On this side of the return of Christ, these seasons are not simply held out as possibilities. They are promised to us. Perhaps you are suffering in such a season—laboring simply to keep your head above water. There are some Sundays, we know, wherein members *barely* make it through the front doors. And on those Sunday mornings wherein you are suffocating with suffering, were you to be asked what *kind* of sermon you think you most need, the *last* thing you would say is, "A sermon on the doctrine of the Trinity." However, it is good to remember that your greatest need that morning, like every morning, is God.

So, while it is not always intuitive, we trust that a heavenward gaze—getting an eyeful of God's glory—is not going to be a waste of time, regardless of what is happening in your life. You may need many things on that hypothetical Sunday morning, but one thing is *most* needful: you need God. Think, then, of this dive into "the depths of God" (c.f., 1 Cor 2:10), as food for your heart. It may not be the meal you are hankering for, but it is healthy for the formation of your soul. We invite you to bank on the sufficiency of God's trinitarian glory this morning. Come, regardless of your problems and worries and anxieties and grief, and simply sit in the presence of God and meditate on his goodness. Heed the invitation of that great Baptist preacher, Charles Spurgeon, who once said:

> Oh, there is, in contemplating Christ, a balm for every wound; in musing on the Father, there is a quietus for every grief; and in the influence of the Holy Ghost, there is a balsam for every sore. Would you lose your sorrow? Would you drown your cares? Then go, plunge yourself in the Godhead's deepest sea; be lost in his immensity; and you shall come forth as from a couch of rest, refreshed and invigorated. I know nothing which can so comfort the soul; so calm the swelling billows of grief and sorrow; so speak peace to the winds of trial, as a devout musing upon the subject of the Godhead.[19]

---

[19] Charles Haddon Spurgeon, "The Immutability of God—Mal. 3:6" in *New Park Street Pulpit,* vol. 1 (1855), public domain.

CHAPTER TWO

The Saving Trinity

Triune Self-Revelation and the Gospel

How does God reveal himself as Trinity? The question is overwhelming. Who among us does not have friends or family members who ask, incredulously, "How can Christians believe that God is one, and that Jesus and the Holy Spirit are God along with the Father?" Even among Christians there is a lot of confusion, misunderstanding, and downright bafflement. Yet we should not despair. Granted, answering this type of question can at first seem almost impossible for the average Christian. One might feel as though there is so much material to go through before even attempting an answer that a failure to launch creeps over him, as if he needs an advanced degree in theology. It all feels overwhelming. And to be fair, what we said in the previous chapter about God's incomprehensibility still stands. It is *right*, in some sense, for those who contemplate the Trinity to feel out of their depth as they do so. Yet the answer to this question—How does God reveal himself as Trinity?—is at the same time rather basic. God reveals himself as Trinity in the gospel. (And if there is anything that should feel "basic" for a Christian, it is the gospel.) The one God—Creator of heaven and earth—sent his Son to be the light of men, to be our propitiation for sins, and to give us life in him. And when our Lord Jesus, the Son of God, ascended to the right hand of God the Father, the Holy Spirit—who is the love of God—was poured out. This is how the triune God was revealed to the human race: the God over all brought salvation to the human race *as Trinity*.

This chapter seeks to uphold this tension between, on the one hand, the overwhelming and transcendent reality that the God who is one is Trinity, and, on the other hand, the gracious truth that we have come to know God as Trinity in the very gospel we came to embrace when we first believed.

The Holy Trinity's self-revelation is *organic* to the Scriptures. In other words, the doctrine of the Holy Trinity is not simply made up of a collection of verses or passages. As we saw in the previous chapter, a robust doctrine of the Trinity is richer than a mere mathematical formula (as if X passages describing God as Father + Y passages describing Christ's divinity + Z passages describing the Spirit's divinity = the doctrine of the Trinity). The temptation to create such a formula comes from an impulse that requires a chapter and verse *explicitly* declaring a doctrine in order for it to be considered truly "biblical." But this kind of theological method is not adequate for biblical *reasoning* because such an approach is incapable of perceiving the whole counsel of God. Scripture invites us not only to positively declare what is explicitly stated but also to draw out what is implicitly present "by good and necessary consequence."[1] In this sense, there is no single proof text for the doctrine of the Trinity—the whole Bible is the Trinity's "proof text," wherein this doctrine organically unfolds along the contours of redemptive history (more on this as the chapter continues). Faith that seeks understanding of the Holy Trinity requires us to read the Bible as a whole and with the *whole* church. While in-depth studies of books or sections of the Bible are appropriate and necessary, we should always read them in light of the whole canon because that is how God has revealed himself.

This chapter will develop in four parts. First, we will discuss how we should *approach* and *read* the Scriptures. This is sometimes grouped under the heading of "prolegomena." And while this includes the technical skills of interpretation and habits of mind, there is an irreducibly spiritual and personal aspect to our methodology that we cannot ignore. If the Scriptures are God's self-revelation and are thereby a means of grace to commune with him, our engagement with them is anything but sterile and distant. We do not read the words as disembodied information processors, indifferent to the object of study, but we always come to the Scriptures as those with a vested interest. Therefore, we are to approach any aspect of Christian theology in humble prayer. This posture aids us to see that God is God and we are not. It also shows us that we only know anything about him because he has stooped to bring himself within our reach—within our creaturely existence. We are hopeless at even making a start at this topic apart from his say so (Heb 6:1–3)! This pronounced difference between us and

---

[1] See Westminster Confession 1.6. For an introductory exploration, see Ryan McGraw, *By Good and Necessary Consequence* (Grand Rapids: Reformation Heritage Books, 2012).

God at the start—between the Creator and the creature, between who God is in himself and how God has revealed himself in time and space—chastises the temptation to imagine that God is circumscribed by what he reveals about himself in history. God is no less than his self-revelation in the gospel, and he is infinitely and incomprehensibly *more*.

Second, we will consider the vexing question of how to think about the Holy Trinity and the Old Testament. Does the Old Testament reveal God as triune? How do we reconcile the difference between the Old Testament's "The LORD our God, the LORD is one" (Deut 6:4) and the New Testament's "in the name of the Father and of the Son and of the Holy Spirit" (Matt 28:19). Here, we will briefly discuss how divine naming in the Old Testament led to the New Testament's interpretation of the Old Testament in light of the incarnation and Pentecost.

Third, we will consider how the interpretation by Jesus and the New Testament writers demonstrates that there is one God Most High existing eternally in three persons. In other words, we will discover that God as the eternal Three-in-One is how Jesus and his apostles *themselves* read the Scriptures. We will see this both through the *events* of the incarnation and Pentecost, and through the biblical *formulas* prescribed and pronounced around liturgical concepts like baptism and doxology.[2]

Fourth, we will look at how the doctrine of the Holy Trinity is *the* principal subject in Christian theology, both theologically and practically. If you get the doctrine of the Trinity wrong, theological trouble awaits you down the road. Sound theology in *any* respect is jeopardized if there is no sound trinitarian theology at the start,

---

[2] Here, the writings of Scott R. Swain and Fred Sanders have been helpful in articulating how God reveals himself as Trinity.

which makes the doctrine of the Trinity the most consequential of doctrines. We may think trinitarian error has no impact on our understanding of the gospel, but it does. For example, consider the songs we sing on the Lord's Day. Lyrics about Christ leaving his Father's throne and emptying himself of all but love seem to be freighted with particular trinitarian ideas.[3] The Trinity is not merely one doctrine among many; it is the very substance of the Christian faith.[4] Indeed, no other doctrine is more important for the Christian life than the Holy Trinity. As the One who is the fountain of life, light, and love, the Trinity *is* the Christian's salvation.

Reading to Participate in the Trinity

The source and subject of Scripture, the Holy Trinity, demands that we approach the task of reading the biblical data in a particular way. When we read the Scriptures, we should engage in humble contemplation that seeks to grow in knowledge of God through faith in Christ by the illumination of the Spirit. Scripture is the source of many joys for the Christian, but the source and subject matter of the Trinity stands above them all. The church father

---

[3] See verse 3 of Charles Wesley's hymn "And Can It Be That I Should Gain?" (1738) on hymnal.net, https://www.hymnal.net/en/hymn/h/296/4.

[4] This is a point that D. A. Carson misses when he questions why a "trinitarian" reading of Scripture should be privileged above any other theological loci. Carson seems to suggest that to insist on making the Trinity theologically central when reading Scripture is arbitrary—as if there were just as much reason for making a theology of "resurrection" or "Christology" or "soteriology" conceptually central as for making a theology of Trinity so. In doing so, he fundamentally fails to situate the Trinity in its rightful dogmatic home. E.g., see D. A. Carson "Theological Interpretation of Scripture: Yes, but . . ." in *Theological Commentary: Evangelical Perspectives*, ed. R. Michael Allen (London: T&T Clark, 2011), 205.

Augustine once said, "And it [Scripture] not only feeds them with the evident truth . . . but so that obvious truths do not become boring, the same truths are again desired as concealed, and as desired are in a sense refreshed, and as refreshed they are taught with sweetness. By these, evil minds are salutarily corrected, little minds are fed, and great minds are delighted."[5] As we encounter the Holy Trinity in the Holy Scriptures, we are corrected of evil, fed by the words of Christ, and delight in the grace poured out by the Spirit. And let us not forget that we are given knowledge of this life-giving subject by grace through faith. The divine blessedness causes preeminent gladness because the life of the Trinity sinks down into our hearts and makes us happy, or in other words, because the life of the Trinity draws us up and we sink into *it* and are made happy. Listen to the words of Asaph in Ps 73:23–26: "I am always with you; you hold my right hand. You guide me with your counsel, and afterward you will take me up in glory. Who do I have in heaven but you? And I desire nothing on earth but you. My flesh and my heart may fail, but God is the strength of my heart, my portion forever." The One who is good *in himself* has descended to make himself known to us, those who are his enemies, *and has thereby* caused us to participate in his eternal fountain of life. The Trinity is the very source of our participation, knowledge, and worship of the Trinity. Nothing on this earth has the ability to give us life, strength, and portion; but God, who is life and goodness himself, is our portion forever. In other words, by the grace of the Trinity, we behold the Trinity in the Scriptures. This is what we mean when we say that the Trinity is not only the *subject* of Holy Scripture, but also its *source*.

---

[5] Augustine, *The Works of Augustine,* part 2, *Letters,* trans. Roland J. Teske, vol. 2, *Letters 100–155* (Hyde Park, NY: New City, 2003), 223.

But in what sense is the doctrine of the Holy Trinity *biblical*? There does not seem to be a single chapter/verse reference to portray all that we intend to communicate in this doctrine.[6] Nevertheless, this does not render the doctrine non-biblical or extra-biblical. There is a deeper sense of what it means for the doctrine of the Trinity to be revealed as a biblical doctrine. While some doctrines can be formulated in a "proof-text" manner, this is not the only way Christians formulate dogma. As Fred Sanders says, "The basic vocabulary of Trinitarian theology is not found on the surface of the text. . . . In the fullness of time, God did not give us facts about himself, but *gave us himself* in the person of the Father who sent, the Son who was sent, and the Holy Spirit who was poured out."[7] We follow well-charted territory when we say with a number of confessions that the whole counsel of God is either expressly set down in Scripture *or by good and necessary consequence* derived from Scripture.

There are some doctrines that are explicitly sitting at the surface of the text, such that you cannot see anything without seeing them—to approach the text is to brush up against the doctrine (*creatio ex nihilo* in Gen 1:1, for example). These doctrines are as conspicuous as the color of paint on the wall in your bedroom. There are other doctrines that are implied by the plain reading of a text, even if not articulated in a propositional statement (such as the doctrine of God's omniscience in Ps 139:2). These doctrines are like the drywall under the paint in your bedroom. But there are still other doctrines that *have* to be true because their falsity would

---

[6] While there may be texts that showcase the existence of the three persons (i.e., Jesus's baptism), it does not demonstrate all that Nicene orthodoxy intends to communicate.

[7] Fred Sanders, *The Triune God* (Grand Rapids: Zondervan, 2016), 39–40; emphasis added.

mean the dissolution of other doctrines in the first two categories. We can call these doctrines load-bearing—they have to be true in order for the whole structure to hold together. The doctrine of the Trinity is such a load-bearing doctrine. Granted, even to affirm this construct, we must presuppose that Christian doctrine is a cohesive whole that is derived (either directly or by good and necessary consequence) from divinely inspired Scripture and across the whole canon. This may be a leap for the unbeliever, but so be it. We are talking about *Christian* doctrine after all.

Once this much has been granted, we may begin to investigate just how the Trinity is a load-bearing doctrine. How can we verify that this doctrine comes from the Scriptures by good and necessary consequence? In brief, here are some principles.[8] First, God interprets himself through Scripture. That is, he reveals himself by giving us himself in word and deed. Thus, we should read our whole Bibles with the whole God. For example, the divine name of Yahweh in the Old Testament and the New Testament's attribution of Jesus and the Holy Spirit as Lord signifies their identification with the One God Most High (Matt 28:19; 1 Cor 8:6; Acts 5:3–4). Unless we are prepared to say that Scripture contradicts itself, we must grant that Yahweh is the divine name given to *One God* (Deut 6:4) who is *three*. If that is *who Yahweh is*, it is *who Yahweh always has been*, which means we are invited to read passages of the three persons in light of the one name, and passages of the one name in light of the three persons (more on this as the chapter continues).

Second, we can look to our Christian tradition as a pedagogue and counselor. There is no such thing as coming to the Bible in a

---

[8] These three notes are condensed for the sake of brevity, but for a more comprehensive guide, see R. B. Jamieson and Tyler R. Wittman, *Biblical Reasoning* (Grand Rapids: Baker Academic, 2022).

state of theological neutrality—that is, with no theological or philosophical presuppositions. We are simply calling you to be honest with yourself, asking for help and receiving the gifts that God has given: his Word, his Spirit, and his *people*. Recall the previous chapter that briefly mentioned how the saints of old worked through these difficult and glorious doctrines long before us. Their work has been handed down to us through the providence of God. This does not mean that all their methods and conclusions are infallible (for only the Scriptures are infallible), only that there is a longstanding history of confessional identity concerning the triune God and how this God has revealed himself. We should not neglect our brothers and sisters of old who labored on these matters. So with the great tradition, we have a wide and broad range of testimony that we should use to "check our work" against, so to speak. While acknowledging the various presentations, the church has generally taken the same data (the Scriptures), worked over the same issues ("How can Yahweh be one while Father, Son, and Spirit are all identified with that one name?"), and has come to the same conclusions (the doctrine of the Trinity) with the same methods (which we will lay out in this chapter). This should give us a clue that we went astray somewhere if we are taking the same data to answer the same questions to reach different conclusions. Tradition is therefore an authority of sorts, even if it is an authority that derives its legitimacy only under the authority of the Scriptures.[9]

---

[9] There is obviously *so much more* to say about the authority of the tradition, but for a cogently argued and accessible presentation of the view we describe here, see J. V. Fesko, *The Need for Creeds Today: Confessional Faith in a Faithless Age* (Grand Rapids: Baker Academic, 2020), 1–18. See also, Craig A. Carter, *Interpreting Scripture with the Great Tradition: Recovering the Genius of Premodern Exegesis* (Grand Rapids: Baker Academic, 2018); Gavin Ortlund, *Theological Retrieval for Evangelicals: Why We Need Our*

Third, the God we encounter and experience through the Scriptures, we experience *as* Trinity. This principle is a bit more complex than the other two, so let us recruit some help from the family heritage described above. Basil of Caesarea comments on the twofold path or way of our approach to the mystery of the Trinity: "The way to divine knowledge ascends from one Spirit through the one Son to the one Father. Likewise, natural goodness, inherent holiness and royal dignity reaches from the Father through the Only-Begotten to the Spirit."[10] The first way to divine knowledge, which is largely what concerns us in this chapter, is what we experience. Our race of faith begins as the Holy Spirit enlightens and illumines our minds to the glory of the Son to behold the Father. The Holy Spirit regenerates us. And that term *regenerate* means far more than we can comprehend because he is transferring us from the kingdom of darkness to the kingdom of the beloved Son where we participate in the divine life. That is salvation: united to Christ we enjoy communion with the Holy Trinity. Gilles Emery comments on this first path of our experience: "The Holy Spirit is Gift in person: it is in him that believers are able to know the Son and to have access to the Father. In baptism, believers are consecrated to the Father through the Son, in the Holy Spirit who accomplishes interiorly their regeneration."[11] The God we meet in the Scriptures is

---

Past to Have a Future (Wheaton, IL: Crossway, 2019); Michael Allen and Scott R. Swain, *Reformed Catholicity: The Promise of Retrieval for Theology and Biblical Interpretation* (Grand Rapids: Baker Academic, 2015).

[10] Basil of Caesarea, *On the Holy Spirit* (Crestwood, NY: St. Vladimir's Press, 2011), 18.47:74–75.

[11] Gilles Emery, *The Trinity: An Introduction to Catholic Doctrine on the Triune God*, trans. Matthew Levering (Washington, DC: Catholic University of America Press, 2011), 11.

experienced when God the Holy Spirit regenerates us and unites us to God the Son, who leads us into fellowship with God the Father.

The second path of contemplating the mystery of the Trinity is from above, that is, within the life of God himself. The Father eternally communicates the fullness of the divine essence to the Son in eternal generation and to the Holy Spirit through the Son in eternal spiration. Thus, the eternal and perfect life of God exists in Father, Son, and Spirit. Such an affirmation impresses on us the importance of distinguishing between what theologians used to call *theologia* and *oikonomia*, that is, God *ad extra* and God *ad intra*, or what has more recently been called the "ontological" or "immanent Trinity" and the "economic Trinity."

There is a distinction we need to make between the eternal life of God in himself and what God does in the history of salvation. We must not conflate or confuse the temporal missions (e.g., how the Father sends his Son) with the eternal processions. "The economy does not constitute the Holy Trinity. In other words, the Father does not become Father by his relation with us in Christ . . . the eternal life of God is necessary (since he is the Creator and Fountain of life), whereas the economy is not . . . we should not conflate the reality of the Trinity in himself, in his transcendent mystery, with the human knowledge and experience that we can have of the Trinity."[12] We are limited creatures receiving knowledge of our infinite Creator. So by nature, our knowledge and language of him is necessarily proportionate to who we are by nature. Calvin is famous for describing this God-talk as "lisping."[13] God anthropomorphizes himself with his self-communication in creation and redemption

---

[12] Emery, 177.

[13] John Calvin, *Institutes of the Christian Religion*, ed. John T. McNeill, trans. Ford Lewis Battles (Louisville: WJK, 1960), 1.13.1.

because those to whom he reveals himself are *anthropos* (Greek for "human")—he speaks to us and reveals himself to us in ways that we can understand. The infinite can be communicated truly to the finite, but never in such a way that the infinite is circumscribed by the finite.

If the created economy *exhausted* the eternal life of God, there would be no mystery, and God would not be God. Since God is perfect in his incomprehensible beauty, our language for God is given to us by God in analogous form. God's revelation of himself in the history of salvation gives us *true* access to knowledge of God but not in such a way as to comprehensively fit the infinite into the finite. When we remember who we are and who God is by contrast, we can approach his self-revelation with humility. On the one hand, we will be spared from the danger of assuming that God is *constituted* by his acts in history, as if he were a mere creature living side by side with us. On the other hand, we will be spared from the danger of concluding that his acts in history reveal nothing at all of who he is in himself. God is no less than what he reveals himself to be in history, but he is infinitely *more*. The purpose of God's revelation of himself in the economy is our salvation. By the Spirit, we are illumined and enlightened to the beauty of the Son and the blessedness of the Father.

In other words, the *missions* in the economy are fitting in view of the timeless processions because they truly extend and reveal the incomprehensible Trinity. While in different ways, this "fittingness" was important for Athanasius, John of Damascus, and Thomas Aquinas, among others. For Athanasius, the Son's "*homoousios* with" carries the same reality as the language used in the book of Hebrews—"image of" and "radiance of."[14] The Son is eternally generated by the

---

[14] On the "derivative nature" of *homoousios* in Athanasius, see R. P. C. Hanson, *The Search for the Christian Doctrine of God: The Arian Controversy 318–381* (Grand Rapids: Baker Academic, 2005), 443.

Father who is unbegotten. Thus, it is fitting that the Son is the one who is sent. For John of Damascus, in the mystery of the incarnation, God's power and wisdom is proclaimed because the one conquered now becomes the Conqueror, and "he found the most fitting solution for this most difficult problem."[15] With wisdom and power being appropriated to God the Son (1 Cor 1:24), it was fitting that God the Son become incarnate. Finally, for Thomas Aquinas, the Holy Spirit is seen as the Gift of the Father and the Son since "the remission of sins is accomplished by the Holy Spirit as the Gift of God,"[16] poured into our hearts. At both Jesus's baptism and Pentecost, we see the visible mission of the Spirit as fitting in view of his timeless procession from the Father and the Son.

Trinity and the Old Testament

With the above principles set in place, how does the doctrine of the Trinity fit with the Old Testament Scriptures? We must state up front that the Old Testament does not reveal the Trinity in the same manner as the New Testament. We must remember that for God's people, divine revelation occurred across many centuries and through many individuals. This is what we mean by the term "progressive revelation." And this is what Gal 4:4–7 makes clear: "But when the fullness of time had come, God sent forth his Son, born of woman, born under the law, to redeem those who were under the law, so that we might receive adoption as sons. And because you are sons, God has sent the Spirit of his Son into our

---

[15] John of Damascus, *On the Orthodox Faith 3.1*, in *The Fathers of the Church: John of Damascus: Writings*, trans. Fredrick H. Chase Jr., vol. 37 (Washington, DC: Catholic University of America Press, 1999), 268.

[16] Thomas Aquinas, *Summa Theologiae*, vol. 48, *The Incarnate Word: 3a, 1–6* (Cambridge: Cambridge University Press, 2006), 3a.3.8.

hearts, crying, 'Abba, Father!' So you are no longer a slave, but a son, and if a son, then an heir through God" (ESV).

However, this fact does not reduce our comments regarding the Trinity in the Old Testament to silence. This is because the "fullness of time" designates, for Paul, a culmination of redemptive history that dates back to the Old Testament. God's work in the Old Testament was *always* intended to conclude in his triune self-revelation in the New. This is why Paul, in the same context of his letter to the Galatians, can go so far as to say that "the Scripture, foreseeing that God would justify the Gentiles by faith, *preached the gospel beforehand to Abraham*, saying, 'In you shall all the nations be blessed'" (Gal 3:8 ESV; emphasis added). In this sense, Christ himself was the promised seed of Abraham (Gal 3:16). But the story of the gospel and the revelation of the Trinity coinhere with one another—the latter happens *by* the former. So to whatever degree the Old Testament speaks to and signals the gospel, it speaks to and signals the Trinity. Therefore, we can say that when the Old Testament speaks of the salvation of sinners, it speaks of the Trinity, and vice versa. Without conflating the history of salvation onto God in himself, we are on the true biblical path of contemplating the Trinity through our salvation. We can "recognize that while the Trinity was not yet clearly revealed in the time of the Old Testament, the reality of the Trinity is signaled in those texts precisely as much as the gospel itself is, 'preached beforehand' because its results are 'foreseen' by Scripture itself."[17]

B. B. Warfield gives us another metaphor for the Trinity in the Old Testament. There we walk into a dimly lit room where we can barely make out the scope of the room, bumping into furniture along the way, but without any idea that it is furniture. But over

---

[17] Sanders, *The Triune God*, 45.

time, the room gets brighter so that we can actually see the scope of the room and its furniture.[18] In the same way, the OT is dimly lit, but with Christ's incarnation and the Spirit's being poured out, we're able to see that God did not *become* triune with the incarnation and Pentecost. No, the God who is one has eternally existed as Father, Son, and Spirit. What appears different to us is the manner in which God has worked out our salvation in the fullness of time! This is another way of stating what we have affirmed already: in our redemption we receive true revelation of the Holy Trinity. And with that revelation we have redemption in him. This gives even more substance to the faithfulness of God to fulfill his promises to the Old Testament people of God. He was not merely keeping his word; he kept his word *by giving us himself.*

So that is one way of categorizing the Trinity and the Old Testament, but another important category (and one we have mentioned already) has everything to do with divine naming in the Old Testament (and, subsequently, how the New Testament writers interpret Old Testament divine naming in light of the incarnation and Pentecost). Scott Swain helpfully summarizes the mystery of the Trinity in the Old Testament:

> The Old Testament speaks of the Trinity, portraying God as a sovereign speech agent who created all things by his Word and Spirit (Gen. 1:1–3; Ps. 33:6, 9), inviting us to overhear conversations between the Lord and his anointed Son (Ps. 2; 110), and prompting us to wonder about the threefold repetition of YHWH's name in the Aaronic

---

[18] Benjamin Breckinridge Warfield, "The Biblical Doctrine of the Trinity," in *The Works of Benjamin B. Warfield*, vol. 2, *Biblical Doctrines* (New York: Oxford University Press, 1932; repr., Grand Rapids: Baker, 2003), 141–42.

Benediction (Num. 6:22–27; 2 Sam. 23:2–3) and about the true identity of Wisdom in Proverbs 8.[19]

Here, the divine name of Yahweh beckons contemplation, posing a conundrum that only ultimately concludes with the revelation of the New Testament.

The New Testament writers demonstrate how we are to understand the odd and unclear texts of the Old Testament where multiple speakers are present.[20] For example, Gen 1:1–3 with John 1:1–3; or Psalm 2 with Hebrews 1; or Psalm 110 and Isa 49:3 with Mark 12:35–37; or Mic 5:2–4 with Matt 2:15. Where the Old Testament designates speakers as literary personifications or leaves them unidentified, the New Testament identifies Wisdom and Word as God's eternal Son. Though the New Testament does not utilize the term "person" to describe the Father, Son, or Spirit, it does designate the speakers as persons by means of their dialogue with one another. Scholars call this "prosopological exegesis," and it has strong explanatory power to otherwise befuddling texts.[21]

It may be helpful to think about God's works and how Scripture exercises person-analogies to demonstrate God's triune nature and

---

[19] Scott R. Swain, *The Trinity: An Introduction* (Wheaton: Crossway, 2020), 25.

[20] We are following Scott R. Swain, "Divine Trinity," in *Christian Dogmatics: Reformed Theology for the Church Catholic* (Grand Rapids: Baker Academic, 2016); and Matthew W. Bates, *The Birth of the Trinity: Jesus, God, and Spirit in New Testament and Early Christian Interpretations of the Old Testament* (Oxford: Oxford University Press, 2016) here.

[21] For more on prosopological exegesis and the historical precedent, see Bates, *The Birth of the Trinity*; John Behr, *The Way to Nicaea* (New York: St. Vladimir's, 2001); and Madison Pierce, *Divine Discourse in the Epistle to the Hebrews: The Recontextualization of Spoken Quotations in Scripture* (Cambridge: Cambridge University Press, 2020).

agency. "Scripture portrays God as a sovereign King who speaks the world into existence by his sovereign Word and Spirit (Ps. 33:6). Scripture portrays God as a father who sends a beloved son on a mission to gather the fruits of his vineyard (Mark 12:1–12)."[22] And Scripture portrays God as Redeemer who sends his Spirit to give life and adoption (Gal 4:4–7). We will delve more into what is called inseparable operation and divine appropriations in later chapters but suffice it to say here that the New Testament writers interpret Old Testament texts in trinitarian fashion through person-speaker interpretation and through the divine salvific agency of Father, Son, and Spirit.

Let us see what this looks like by considering the example of one of the Old Testament's most important developments: God's self-naming in Exod 3:14 and his exposition of it in Exod 34:6–7. In Exodus 3, God reveals to Moses the name *Yahweh*, which signals many divine aspects for Moses. The Reformed theologian Francis Turretin notes three implications: (1) God is eternal and independent such that he is necessary and self-existent, (2) God is the first and most perfect being that is the first and final cause, and (3) God is immutable and constant.[23] Moses physically sees this in the burning bush. We know that fire needs oxygen to exist, yet God is life in himself such that he requires nothing outside of himself to exist. This fire can burn without consuming the bush because it existed independent of the bush. Moreover, as we see in

---

[22] Swain, *The Trinity: An Introduction*, 108–9.

[23] Francis Turretin, *Institutes of Elenctic Theology*, vol. 1 (Phillipsburg: P&R, 1992), 3.4.5. While the point of this section is not to examine the fullness of exegetical realities behind the mysterious scene of Exodus 3, for those readers who wish to explore this further, see Andrea Saner, *Too Much to Grasp: Exodus 3:13–15 and the Reality of God* (University Park: Eisenbrauns, 2015).

Exod 34:6–7, Yahweh signals perfection and immutability as the basis for his covenant faithfulness in grace and truth.

Now, in light of this, let us consider John 1:1–14. Our attention is drawn to John 1:14 primarily because of the use of *charis* (grace) and *alētheia* (truth). Here, under the guidance of the Holy Spirit, John recalls Exod 34:6–7 where Yahweh reveals his glory and character to Moses. There are a number of significant parallels between Exodus 33–34 and John 1:14–18: Israel finds grace in Yahweh's sight (Exod 33:14), and the disciples receive "grace upon grace" (John 1:16); Yahweh's glory passes by Moses (Exod 33:23; 34:6–7), and the disciples beheld the Word's glory (John 1:14); Yahweh abounds in grace and truth (Exod 34:6), and Jesus is full of grace and truth (John 1:14); Yahweh dwelt in a tent (Exod 33:7), and the Word "tented" among the disciples (John 1:14); Moses is mediator between Yahweh and Israel (Exod 34:32–35), and Jesus is mediator between God and man (John 1:17–18).[24] In other words, because Jesus is the eternal Word-Son, he fulfills the covenant made with the people of God as true Son, and he reveals the glory of God as full of grace and truth. Now, God has "set up his tent" or "made his dwelling" among men in the person of Jesus Christ. Jesus, the eternal Word who eternally existed as God, is the means by which creation and new creation are spoken into existence.

In John 1, there is a clear referral to Exodus 33–34, where Yahweh manifests his glory to Moses through his name, I AM WHO I AM, which he gave in Exod 3:14. D. A. Carson notes, "The glory revealed to Moses when the Lord passed in front of him and sounded his name, displaying that divine goodness characterized by ineffable grace and truth, was the very same glory

---

[24] Andreas Köstenberger, *Encountering John*, Encountering Biblical Studies (Grand Rapids: Baker, 2013), 42.

John and his friends saw in the Word-made-flesh."[25] God has made his covenant faithfulness known in the person of Jesus Christ, who is full of grace and truth. And as we have noted several times over, the revelation of the glory of God reveals the salvation of man: God himself.

Because of this, God's covenant name *Yahweh* and his attribute of divine aseity must be understood in trinitarian language. Divine aseity actually ensures that God is not stoically needless or absent; rather, God is life in and of himself—Father, Son, and Spirit— bringing sinners into that life.[26] The Son, through whom all things were created, is sent by the Father to be our Mediator and to accomplish our salvation. And the Spirit is poured out as he applies the Son's work of redemption and brings us into communion with the Father. The self-existent One gives a common existence to humanity, and in the gospel, he gives salvific existence to his bride. The One *who is*, is our life, the One in whom we live.

Events and Formulas

Now that we have considered the progressive nature of divine revelation, our enlightenment of the Holy Trinity by the Spirit, and the New Testament writers' person-speaker interpretation

---

[25] D. A. Carson, *The Gospel According to John*, PNTC (Grand Rapids: Eerdmans, 1990), 129; cf. Calvin who says, "He had in himself the fulfillment of all things which belong to the spiritual kingdom of God; and, in short, that in all things he showed himself to be the Redeemer and Messiah; which is the most striking mark by which he ought to be distinguished from all others." *Calvin's Commentaries: XVII: Harmony of Matthew, Mark, Luke, John 1–11* (Grand Rapids: Baker, 2009), 48.

[26] Michael Allen, "Divine Attributes," in *Christian Dogmatics: Reformed Theology for the Church Catholic*, ed. Michael Allen and Scott R. Swain (Grand Rapids: Eerdmans, 2016), 65.

of Old Testament passages, we turn to more direct trinitarian constructions in the New Testament. In the New Testament, we see that the writers give us more than trinitarian interpretations of Old Testament promises and perplexing passages. They also give us *formulas:* blessings, doxologies, and divine commands. Each of these formulas is rooted within the events of the incarnation and Pentecost. What God has done in redemptive history, for the New Testament authors, should shape the way we talk about him. As we have noted several times, "When the New Testament speaks of the Trinity, it speaks of the salvation of human beings; and when it speaks of salvation, it speaks of the Trinity."[27]

The New Testament writers were inspired by the Spirit to write about the missions of the Son and Spirit (incarnation and Pentecost) in a way that reveals and relates to the divine being itself. The eternal relations "are *revealed* in the great acts by which redemption is achieved; that they are revealed implies that they already existed."[28] It might be helpful to think about it in terms of God leading us to his invisible triunity through his visible acts in salvation history.[29] As Paul says in Gal 4:4, "When the fullness of time had come" (ESV). The Son was sent by the Father to procure salvation for us, and the Spirit descended on Christ at his baptism (and was poured out on us to know and worship him). By these missions, the invisible is made visible.

As a result of the visible revealing the invisible, the New Testament writers construct trinitarian formulas of God's personal names such as the baptismal formula and the doxological formula.

---

[27] Emery, *The Trinity*, 12.

[28] R. W. Dale, *Christian Doctrine* (London: Hodder & Stoughton, 1894), 151.

[29] Emery, *The Trinity*, 179.

"God's name discloses his personal character and quiddity . . . ; it is therefore the distinguishing mark by which he blesses his people . . . and by which he is blessed."[30] So it is no wonder that these formulas express the eternal reality of the Holy Trinity as they are all numbered or grouped together. The baptismal text, on the one hand, identifies the equality of divinity, the distinction, and the unity of the Holy Trinity, and on the other hand, tells us of the divine life in which we participate. Christ commands his disciples to go and make disciples of all nations, "baptizing them in the name of the Father and of the Son and of the Holy Spirit" (Matt 28:19). There is one name the nations are to be baptized into: the Father, Son, and Holy Spirit. To be baptized into the Father, Son, and Holy Spirit, is to be baptized into Yahweh. They are not three gods or even three parts of one god. Rather, there is one God Most High, Creator of heaven and earth, and he eternally exists as Father, Son, and Holy Spirit. This brings together totalizing passages of Scripture cohesively: no one knows the Father except the Son (Matt 11:27) and no one can say Jesus is Lord except in the Holy Spirit (1 Cor 12:3). God discloses himself in triune-naming fashion.

Likewise, with the doxological formulas, we are told of the way in which our salvation is accomplished. Consider the benediction of 2 Cor 13:13: "The grace of the Lord Jesus Christ, and the love of God, and the fellowship of the Holy Spirit be with you all." Here, we come full circle back to our original statement about approaching and reading the Scriptures in light of trinitarian doctrine. Our path of experience is from the Spirit through the Son to the Father. The doxological formulas articulate this mediatorial access that we have in the blessed life of the Trinity. We are adopted as heirs and commune with the Trinity *through* the grace of Christ,

---

[30] Swain, "Divine Trinity," 83.

in the love of God, and *by* fellowship of the Spirit. We could say much the same of other biblical doxologies, like 1 Cor 8:6; 12:4–6; Eph 4:4–6; and Gal 4:4–7. Basil helpfully summarizes: "If we are illumined by divine power, and fix our eyes on the beauty of the image of the invisible God, and through the image are led up to the indescribable beauty of its source, it is because we have been inseparably joined to the Spirit of knowledge. He gives those who love the vision of truth the power which enables them to see the image, and this power is Himself. He does not reveal it to them from outside sources, but leads them to knowledge personally."[31]

Implications for the Christian Life

As we draw this chapter to a close, let us consider three implications for the Christian life. First, we should take heart in the perfect life of God who acts in creation as he is in himself. The Holy Trinity has revealed his invisible trinitarian glory visibly, through the missions of the incarnation and Pentecost. Consider how grand, wondrous, and perfect God Most High is. Without revealing himself, we have zero hope, security, and life. Thus, it is right and good that we spend considerable time on the blessed mystery of the Trinity, for he is our salvation. If we get trinitarian doctrine wrong, all else crumbles. We must always remember and be awestruck by the fact that the God we approach through the visible self-revealing acts of his redemption in time is *infinitely more* than we can ever understand or comprehend. Remembering this keeps us both grateful for what God has revealed, humbled by the fact that no amount of revelation will or ever could allow us to wrap our minds around it. God will never cease to be a mystery to us. This should

---

[31] Basil of Caesarea, *On the Holy Spirit,* 18.47.

not be a reason for discouragement, since, as Herman Bavinck says, "Mystery is the lifeblood of dogmatics."[32] It is just as true to say that "mystery is the lifeblood of *worship*."

Second, we should keep in mind that it is a false dichotomy to pit theology and practical Christianity against one another, as if preaching and applying the gospel is strictly practical and thinking on the Trinity is strictly intellectual. Indeed, the Christian life is contemplating God and all things in relation to God. Contemplating the perfection of God is the most practical thing you can do, and living virtuously is the most theological thing you can do. This is why Paul concludes Romans 11 with the excellency of God's infinite being: "For from him and through him and to him are all things. To him be glory forever." God is the pillar of our faith, the One who prompts our comfort, the One who incites our piety, and the One who marks true religion. Let us be stirred to worship when we consider that this triune God did not stand afar off, aloof and indifferent to our alienation and estrangement from him, or our ignorance of him. He has revealed his triune nature in a redemptive sweep, by which we are swept up into the blessed life of God himself. If we ought to be amazed and filled with gratitude by the reality of God's saving us in the gospel (and we should), we ought to be amazed and filled with wonder by God's triunity, for there is no having the former without the latter.

Third, we should keep in mind the fact that our growth in the knowledge of the Trinity comes through communion with the Trinity. This is Paul's prayer at the beginning of Col 1:9–14. *Because* we have been transferred into the kingdom of the beloved

---

[32] Herman Bavinck, *Reformed Dogmatics*, vol. 2, *God and Creation*, ed. John Bolt, trans. John Vriend (Grand Rapids: Baker Academic, 2004), 29.

Son, we are equipped to walk in a manner worthy of the Lord by growing in our knowledge of him. And this communion is not a generic communion with a vague sense of the divine—we have communion with the Father, Son, and Spirit. This is such a marvelous subject that the Puritan John Owen wrote a whole book on the topic! In short, we have communion with the One God through each person's gracious work of redemption. "We have communion with the Father in love, communion with the Son in grace, and communion with the Spirit in consolation."[33] Because God has revealed himself as triune in the gospel, and because we only know and encounter this triune God once we are swept up into his work of redemption, contemplation of his triunity cannot be cold or detached. Our contemplation of the Trinity is only fruitful if it is attached to the vine of our communion with the Trinity.

---

[33] Swain, "Divine Trinity," 105

CHAPTER THREE

One God in Trinity
Divine Simplicity in Trinitarian Perspective

One God in Trinity and Trinity in Unity: Retrieving the Athanasian Creed

In the church today, we are experiencing a strange disconnect between doctrine and doxology. We would not have to look long to discover that our lack of liturgy reveals a doctrinal void. Likewise, songs written for the purpose of doxology are almost entirely devoid of theological content. That disconnect may explain, in part at least, why the doctrine of the Trinity appears to be so absent from the life and soul of the church. Contemplating the Trinity in the church is a strange practice for pastors and churchgoers alike. The gospel they know. Discipleship they know. But the Trinity is a stranger in their midst.

However, the church was not always a vacancy for contemplating the Trinity. For example, consider the Athanasian Creed. Although the creed is named after the church father Athanasius, who defended the Nicene Creed against the subordination of the Son, the creed itself was not written by Athanasius but by his successors in the Western church. The church embraced this creed to teach Christians orthodoxy so that they may properly worship God. In the Middle Ages the creed became a key component of the church's liturgy as well. Christians not only sung the psalms but the Athanasian Creed.

By the time of the Reformation, Martin Luther followed those before him when he told churches in Germany to recite the creeds and even sing them together, the Athanasian Creed included. To encourage them, Luther published the creeds in German, so that the church could learn, proclaim, and sing them in their own language. The creeds should be "kept, read, and sung in the whole church, so that I may again bear witness that I hold to the real Christian Church," exclaimed Luther.[1] The Athanasian Creed, therefore, has been central to the church catholic, cultivating sound doctrine and galvanizing true worship for over a millennium.

How instructional, then, for the creed to place an unequivocal emphasis on the unity of the Trinity and the indivisibility of the divine essence (or substance)! With this striking sentence the creed begins, "We worship one God in Trinity and the Trinity in unity, neither confounding their persons nor dividing the essence."[2] On the basis of this indivisibility, the creed can distinguish each person without forfeiting their one essence or substance. For example, the creed reads:

> Thus the Father is Lord,
> the Son is Lord,
> the Holy Spirit is Lord;
> yet there are not three lords, there is but one Lord.

---

[1] Martin Luther, *The Three Symbols or Creeds of the Christian Faith*, in *Luther's Works* (Philadelphia: Fortress, 1960), 34:201.

[2] Chad Van Dixhoorn, *Creeds, Confessions, and Catechisms: A Reader's Edition* (Wheaton, IL: Crossway, 2022), 21.

The creed then explains why:

> Just as Christian truth compels us to confess each person individually as both God and Lord, so catholic religion forbids us to say that there are three gods or lords.

The Athanasian Creed finds an ally in the apostle Paul. Writing to the church in Corinth, Paul must confront a complex dilemma: Should Christians eat food offered to idols? For our purposes, what is so telling is not so much Paul's answer but the *way* he answers. "About eating food sacrificed to idols, then, we know that 'an idol is nothing in the world,' and that 'there is no God but one'" (1 Cor 8:4). Behind Paul's words are the words of Moses. For example, in Deut 4:35, Moses forbids idolatry because, as Israel knew well from the law, the Lord their God, the Lord is one. When Israel was tempted to worship the idols of the surrounding nations, Moses warned, "There is no other besides [the Lord]." According to Moses, the doctrine of God results either in true worship or idolatry.

However, Paul does not merely regurgitate Moses's command but reads Moses's command through Christian spectacles. "For even if there are so-called gods, whether in heaven or on earth . . . yet for us there is one God, the Father. All things are from him, and we exist for him. And there is one Lord, Jesus Christ. All things are through him, and we exist through him" (1 Cor 8:5–6). Paul's words are truly blasphemous if they are not true. Paul has repeated Israel's confession by professing that there is one God and that this God is one, but to include Jesus Christ appears to be a violation of Israel's monotheism.

However, Paul does not believe he has turned one God into two. Paul is persuaded he is justified to reference one Lord who is none other than Father *and* Son. And should we take his second letter to the Corinthians in view, he will include the Holy Spirit as well, saying our sanctification comes "from the Lord who is the Spirit" (2 Cor 3:18). On this basis, the Athanasian Creed can refer to each person of the Trinity as Lord *and* say in the same breath, "There is one Lord." What appears to be a contradiction is a license because these three persons subsist in the same, single divine essence, an essence that cannot be "divided," says the creed.

Whether it be the apostle Paul or the Athanasian creed, both contend that unless the Trinity is indivisible in essence, true worship—and with it, the Christian faith itself—is compromised.[3]

The "God-ness" of God: Simplicity

When the Athanasian Creed warns against "dividing the substance," it assumes the *simplicity* of the Trinity. Today we use words like *simple* and *simplicity* to say something is basic, not difficult to comprehend, or detached from clutter and complications. But the word *simplicity* means something different in theology. When we say God is simple, we mean God is *without parts.*

As created, finite creatures, we are composed beings, and our being is composed of parts. Different parts constitute what it means to be human. For example, we are a composition of body and soul. And even body and soul are composed of their own parts. For instance, the human body is composed of a heart and a brain, lungs and veins, and much more. Parts also define the soul. To describe the substance of the soul in a meaningful way is to speak

---

[3] Notice the Athanasian Creed's concluding sentence: "So in everything . . . the unity in Trinity, and Trinity in unity, is to be worshiped. Anyone who desires to be saved should think thus about the Trinity. . . . This is the catholic faith: that one cannot be saved without believing it firmly and faithfully."

of the intellect, will, and affections. Each part of a human person is essential too, which means we depend on these parts to be complete human beings. No one part is the whole of who we are, but the whole of who we are could not be without these parts.

Parts say a lot about our limitations as well. First, parts mean we have been created. We need someone greater to compose us—to put us together. We are not self-existent. In a day of naturalism and skepticism, we cannot take this profound truth for granted: as compositional beings, man was first made by his Creator.

Second, parts mean we are dependent beings. We are not self-sufficient. If we need someone to compose our parts, then our parts logically precede our being. We rely on our parts *to be*. Otherwise, we cannot be in the first place, let alone function how we should. As the apostle Paul said, "We live and move and have our being" in God, our Creator (Acts 17:28).

Third, parts mean we may pursue certain attributes we desire, but we are not necessarily identical with those attributes. For example, even if we fail to live in a way that is prudent or loving, we cannot change the fact that we are human beings by nature. We may even treat others in inhumane ways—God forbid!—but the fact that we do so as human beings does not change.

Fourth, parts have the potential to change. Each one of us has potential that needs to be actualized to become something more, someone who reaches fulfillment and perfection. We are defined by a passive potency, which means we can be acted on, even modified, as we move from potency to actuality.[4] Compounded by parts, we

---

[4] Passive potency is "the principle which receives change from another" and the "capacity to receive, to be acted on, to be modified." Bernard Wuellner, *Dictionary of Scholastic Philosophy* (Fitzwilliam, NH: Loreto, 2012), 94.

have the potential to *become* something else, for better or worse. We know as much by experience: with time our parts stop working as well as they once did. Once a professor's intellect was brilliant, but now it is plagued by Alzheimer's. Once an athlete's heart pumped with each new stride, but now it suffers from heart disease. With each new succession of moments, all that is made up of parts has the potential to fall apart. On the one hand, we have nothing to be ashamed of when we acknowledge we are made up of parts. Parts are not evil by design (though they certainly have the potential to be corrupted). On the other hand, parts are a true indicator that we are creatures, like a curtain that unveils our finitude.

But God is without parts. He is simple for a variety of reasons: First, God alone is a Creator who is himself without a creator. As the First Cause, he is without a cause. For he alone has life in and of himself (aseity or *a se* in Latin). Self-existent and self-sufficient, he could create this world out of nothing and do so out of pure generosity alone, out of no need in himself.

Second, if God has life in and of himself, then he relies on nothing and no one, including parts, lest those parts precede his being. All that is created exists *by participation*—"In him we live and move and have our being." But God exists *by nature*. He participates in no one because his essence is his existence.[5]

Third, if God exists by nature (essence), then his attributes are not parts of him, but his essence and his attributes are one and the same. All that is in God *is* God. God does not have love; he *is* love. God does not have holiness; he *is* holiness. God does not have power; he *is* all-powerful. In other words, God's essence is

---

[5] "The substance [essence] of God is therefore his existence." Thomas Aquinas, *Summa Theologiae* (Cambridge: Cambridge University Press, 1976; 2006), 1a.3.4.

his attributes and his attributes his essence.[6] This third point is hard for us to understand because our finite minds must parse out God's attributes to consider them at all. But we dare not assume our intellectual limitations mean God—who is without measure—is made up of parts, as if his attributes are not identical with one another but portions of his divisible being. As John Owen clarifies, "*The attributes of God,* which alone seem to be distinct things in the essence of God, *are all of them essentially the same with one another,* and every one the same with the essence of God itself."[7]

Fourth, if God is without time or change, then he must be without parts. For parts, as we said, have the potential to change, for better or worse, always *becoming* something more, something less. But if God is the fullness of everlasting life in and of himself, timeless and unchanging, then he is complete in every way. Maximally alive in the abundance of his infinite life, we can call him pure act.[8] He is not becoming, which implies something is lacking. He is, rather, perfect being. Therefore, God is not simple because he decided to become simple. Simplicity is not something God chooses to be one day. Rather, it's who he is. For God to be God, he cannot be a compositional being. Simplicity, therefore, is the "God-ness" of God.

---

[6] Or we could say, God is without *accidents*. "It is a key claim of divine simplicity that God is not composed of substance and accidents. The reason is that accidents determine a subject to some further actuality that it does not possess in virtue of its substance alone." James Dolezal, "Trinity, Simplicity, and God's Personal Relations," *International Journal of Systematic Theology* 16.1 (2014), 81.

[7] John Owen, *Vindicae Evangelicae,* in *The Works of John Owen,* ed. William Goold (1850–1853; repr., Edinburgh: Banner of Truth Trust), 12:72.

[8] Pure act is "simple perfection . . . without imperfection; mere perfection free of potency." Wuellner, *Dictionary,* 3.

The Persons Are Not Parts

In the age of the church fathers, divine simplicity proved indispensable. Without it they did not believe they could defend orthodoxy from heresy. But why?

The church fathers understood that simplicity justifies our Christian belief in monotheism. Monotheism is the heartbeat of the Hebrew Scriptures, laced across the Old Testament to distinguish true worship from idolatry. Every Hebrew child memorized the greatest commandment: "You shall love the LORD your God with all your heart and with all your soul and with all your might" (Deut 6:5 ESV). But they memorized the previous verse as well: "Hear, O Israel: The LORD our God, the LORD is one" (6:4). The *Shema* warned Israel against her constant temptation to worship the gods of the surrounding nations—nations that did not hesitate to worship more than one god, creating a rivalry of deities. But the *Shema* also reminded Israel why she worshipped one God instead of many gods: Yahweh is not only the one true God, but this God is one. If Yahweh, like the gods of the nations, must share his glory with other gods, even compete with other gods, then he is not the supreme divine being. Someone else outside of himself has divinity too, which means divinity is divided across the spectrum of gods. If divinity is divided, then Yahweh cannot claim to be its sole, simple proprietor. By consequence, he cannot be simple, for he does not have the fullness of divinity in himself—he is not *wholly* God. Simplicity, therefore, proved to be a key pillar in the preservation of Christianity.

Simplicity also defined the type of monotheism compatible with Christianity and its belief in the Trinity. For example, Gregory of Nazianzus clarified monotheism when he said it cannot be "defined as the sovereignty of a single person." If it is, then we never move beyond Judaism to Christianity. But if monotheism is "the single rule produced by equality of nature, harmony of will, identity of action, and the convergence towards their source of what springs from unity," then monotheism is compatible with a God who is one essence and three persons. For even "though there is numerical distinction, there is no division in the substance [essence]."[9] As Christians, we do not choose between monotheism and trinitarianism, but we believe they are compatible with one another, even inseparable from one another. If the Father, Son, and Spirit are not one in essence, will, power, glory, and authority, then we forfeit monotheism *and* succumb to tritheism in a single stroke. But simplicity certifies that Father, Son, and Spirit truly are persons, not parts.

To understand why, we should review what distinguishes the persons of the Trinity. Why does Scripture call the Father, *Father*? It's almost too obvious to say. A father is a father because he begets a son. Likewise, Scripture calls the Father, *Father* for that reason: he begets his Son. His relation with regard to the Son is defined by his personal property of *paternity*. However, we are speaking of *God* the Father, so we must differentiate between paternity in our human experience and paternity in the Godhead. For example, you may be a father with a son, but you too are a son because you were begotten by your father. And your father is a son because he was begotten by his father (your grandfather)—and so on. The same cannot be said of God the Father. He begets his Son, but he has no father that begot him. He is *unbegotten*. Unlike the Son, the Father has no eternal relation of *origin* because he is from no one. Or to change our vocabulary, the Father is the *principle* (source) of the Son, but

---

[9] Gregory of Nazianzus, *On God and Christ* (Crestwood, NY: St Vladimir's Seminary Press, 2002), 3.29.3.

the Father himself has no principle—he is the principle without principle.[10] Otherwise, we would no longer have a Trinity because a fourth person would be included (the Father's Father), resulting in two sons in the Godhead instead of one. To avoid a quaternity (as opposed to a Trinity), we must acknowledge that the Father is the origin or principle from which the other persons proceed, but he himself is without origin or principle. That does not mean the Father has priority, as if he is superior to the Son or Spirit. It only means the Father is the eternal provenance from which the other persons proceed.

Second, why does Scripture call the Son, *Son*? Today, society associates many characteristics with fathers and sons. But to be precise, there is but one thing that is required to be a son: a son is son because he is begotten (or generated) from a father. When Scripture says the divine Son is *Son,* it can do so for that reason: the Son is *Son* because he is begotten from the Father. When we consider the Son's eternal relation of origin, it becomes clear that the Son's personal property is *filiation*. However, unlike human sons, the divine Son is not begotten at a certain point, as if he did not exist before. He is begotten, true enough, but he is begotten from *eternity* (see chapter 4). There never has been, is, or will be a point when the Father is not Father and the Son is not Son. While we, as human sons, may pinpoint *when* we were begotten from our human fathers, there never is a point *when* the Son is begotten from his Father. Previously, we said the Father has no relation of origin since he is unbegotten, but the Son does have a relation of origin since he is begotten from the Father. Except, the Son's relation is an *eternal* relation of origin because his generation from the Father is

---

[10] Principle refers to the source from which a person proceeds. Some in the great tradition have used the word "innascibility" to say the same.

timeless. We will return to this mystery, but here is a rule we should not transgress: when describing the begetting of the Son from the Father, we must not project anything finite (time, change, parts, hierarchy, etc.), lest we impose limitations within the Godhead.

Third, why does Scripture call the Spirit, *Spirit*? Scripture uses this name because this is the Spirit who is *spirated* from the Father and the Son.[11] We do not say the Spirit is begotten from the Father; the Spirit is not a second son from the Father. Nor is the Spirit begotten from the Son, which would not only make him a son of the Son but a grandson of the Father. We avoid these bizarre scenarios when we listen to the way Scripture describes the Spirit: the Spirit is *breathed out* by the Father and the Son (see chapter 5). Sometimes the great tradition will use the word "procession" to this end, concluding that the Spirit proceeds from the Father and the Son. As with eternal generation, we must not impose human limitations when speaking of the Spirit's procession. The Holy Spirit is spirated, but the Spirit's spiration is eternal. Just as there never was a time when the Father was without the Son, so there never was a time when the Father and Son were without the Spirit. The Father and Son spirate the Spirit from eternity. Therefore, as we contemplate the Spirit's eternal relation of origin, we discover that the Spirit's personal property is spiration.

Eternal relations of origin alone distinguish the Son from the Father and the Spirit from the Father and the Son. But what unites all three persons so that we can confess with Scripture that God is one? The great tradition has given us a vocabulary to answer that

---

[11] We may distinguish between *active* spiration, which refers to the Father and the Son as the persons who breathe out the Spirit and *passive* spiration, which refers to the Spirit as the person who is breathed out by the Father and the Son. When we refer to the Spirit's personal property, we are referring to the latter, not the former.

question: each person *subsists* in the same, simple divine essence. "What is common to the divine persons is the concept that each one of them subsists in the divine nature," explains Thomas Aquinas, which is why we call the persons *subsisting relations*.[12] Or think of their unity from this perspective: the one, undivided, and simple divine essence has *three modes of subsistence*. "The personal properties [paternity, filiation, spiration] by which the persons are distinguished from the essence are certain modes by which it [the essence] may be characterized," says Reformed theologian, Francis Turretin.[13] In short, a "divine person is nothing but *the divine essence . . . subsisting in an especial manner*," says Puritan John Owen.[14]

Remember, the Father is unbegotten.[15] No one communicates the divine essence to him since he is not begotten nor is he spirated. Rather, he is the One who communicates the divine essence

---

[12] Thomas Aquinas, *Summa Theologiae*, 1a.30.4.

[13] Turretin adds, not "formally and properly" (as with creatures), but "eminently and analogically, all imperfection being removed." He concludes, "Thus the person may be said to differ from the essence not really (*realiter*), i.e., essentially . . . but modally." *Institutes of Elenctic Theology* 1:278. "Mode" is not to be confused with "modalism" but as Dolezal says, elaborating on Turretin, mode merely refers to the "essence's 'manner' of subsistence," that is, its "mode of subsistence." "Trinity," 96.

[14] John Owen, *Brief Vindication*, in *The Works of John Owen*, ed. William H. Goold (Edinburgh: Banner of Truth Trust, 2009), 2:407; emphasis in the original. One of the best treatments of this issue is Dolezal, "Trinity," 94.

[15] In addition, if the Father is not begotten or spirated, then we may say that he is *innascible*, which means he is from no one. He is the Principle who has no principle. However, we should not make the serious mistake of assuming that since he is the Principle, he must have priority, making the Son and Spirit inferior. For a helpful treatment of innascibility, see John Baptist Ku's chapter, "The Unbegotten Father," in *On Classical Trinitarianism: Retrieving the Nicene Doctrine of the Triune God*, ed. Matthew Barrett (Downers Grove, IL: IVP Academic, 2025).

to the Son and with the Son to the Spirit. The Son is begotten from the Father, which distinguishes him as *Son*. Yet the begetting of the Son is not averse to his equality with the Father. For the Son is begotten from the Father's divine *essence*.[16] Although the Son is distinguished by his personal property of filiation, nevertheless, all the perfections of divinity are common properties that belong to the Son due to his eternal generation from the Father's essence. Or consider the Spirit who is breathed out by the Father and the Son. Spiration distinguishes the Spirit from the Father and the Son, yet the Spirit's spiration from the Father and the Son is not opposed to the Spirit's equality with the Father and the Son. From all eternity, the Father and Son communicate the one, simple, undivided divine essence to the Spirit. The Spirit is distinguished by the personal property of spiration, yet all the perfections of divinity are common properties of the Spirit due to the Spirit's eternal spiration from the Father and Son's divine essence.

Here is the critical point: the persons of the Trinity *are* subsisting relations of the same, simple divine essence. "When we speak of the divine persons we are not speaking about something *other* than the divine essence, something adjoined to it," explains James Dolezal. "*Rather, they are simply the divine essence subsisting in a threefold manner.*"[17]

Simplicity: Guardrail for Orthodoxy

Simplicity is like a good fence, a guardrail that keeps us within the bounds of orthodoxy. As we learned in chapter 1, the church

---

[16] Matthew Barrett, *Simply Trinity: The Unmanipulated Father, Son, and Spirit* (Grand Rapids: Baker, 2021), 161.
[17] Dolezal, "Trinity," 94; emphasis in the original.

in the fourth century was shaken by the Arian controversy, a controversy that galvanized the church fathers at the Council of Nicaea.[18] Arians agreed with other church fathers who said God is incomprehensible—no finite creature can comprehend the essence of God. The Arians also agreed with the church fathers when they asserted the timelessness of God—whereas the creature is limited by a succession of moments, the Creator is eternal. Furthermore, the Arians agreed with the church fathers when they said this incomprehensible, eternal God is immutable—unlike finite creatures, the Creator does not change. Moreover, the Arians agreed with the church fathers when they said the incomprehensible, eternal, immutable God is impassible—in contrast to the creature, the Creator is without passions, suffering no change that comes with emotions. However, the church fathers believed these divine perfections were common properties of both the Father and the Son. Arianism, by contrast, could only speak of these perfections with reference to the Father. After all, they said, the Son is brought into existence—at one time the Son was not—which means he cannot comprehend the essence of the Father. And if he is brought into existence by the Father, then he cannot be begotten from eternity. And if he is not begotten from eternity, then how can he be immutable and impassible in nature like the Father?

However, none of these limitations in the Son were disconcerting to the Arians. God cannot connect with a comprehensible, temporal, mutable, and passible creation without defiling his divinity, but what if he became a Father of a Son who could make contact? To

---

[18] To hear Arius in his own words, read his letters in William G. Rusch, ed., *The Trinitarian Controversy* (Philadelphia: Fortress, 1980). To consider how Arianism develops, see Aloys Grillmeier, *Christ in Christian Tradition*, vol. 1, *From the Apostolic age to Chalcedon (451)*, trans. John Bowden (Atlanta: JKP, 1975).

make this happen, however, this Son had to be inferior to the Father but superior to creation, capable of condescending to the point of suffering a passion, even a crucifixion. Behind such a solution sat several assumptions: First, the Son is Son by grace, not by nature. The Arians were, at points, willing to use a word like "God" and "Son" in the same sentence *if* this Son is a second, subordinate deity, dependent on God to live and move and have his being. Still, whatever divine properties are attributed to the Son cannot be his by nature but only by participation. Moreover, there are some properties, such as eternity, immutability, and impassibility, that the Son cannot participate in whatsoever.[19]

Second, if the Son is only a Son by participation—a Son by grace, not by nature—then the unity between the Father and the Son cannot be anything more than a unity of will(s). Again, this assumption underlies the Arian understanding of the Son's relation of origin. As mentioned, the Son is begotten, but he is not begotten from eternity. When God decided to beget a Son (making God a Father), he created his Son *ex nihilo*—out of nothing. However superior the Son may be to angels, humans, and animals, nevertheless, he is still within the created realm, made by the Creator, the Monarch. Since he is external to God, he cannot be begotten from the Father's *essence*. He is only a product of the Father's will. Whatever divinity, glory, honor, or authority define him he has as a gift.

More to the point, whatever *unity* the Son has with his Father cannot be a unity of nature. Such a unity is impossible if the Son is

---

[19] For examples, see R. P. C. Hanson, *The Search for the Christian Doctrine of God: The Arian Controversy, 318–381* (Grand Rapids: Baker Academic, 2006), 114. Also see my forthcoming chapter in Barrett, *On Classical Trinitarianism*.

not eternally begotten but made. By consequence, when Scripture describes the unity between Father and Son, it does not refer to an ontological unity (ontology refers to being or nature or essence) but merely a functional unity (functional referring to a volitional cooperation). But again, the Arians did not consider this difference a weakness, because a mere functional unity is necessary to keep the Creator undefiled from creation. Such reasoning could even sound quite "gospel-centered." The Son is made, not eternally begotten, so that he can be the Mediator between God and all else that has been made. If he is one in nature with God, it may seem, he cannot serve as the intercessor between the Creator and the fallen creation.

Scripture, however, paints a picture of trinitarian unity that cannot be reconciled with subordinationism (e.g., Arianism). For example, consider the words of Jesus during the Festival of Dedication. The festival occurred in Jerusalem during the winter. Jesus decided he would walk in the temple when the Jews spotted him and cornered him. No longer willing to be patient, they demanded he answer their question, "How long are you going to keep us in suspense? If you are the Messiah, tell us plainly" (John 10:24). Apparently, the Jews were not listening with their eyes, because Jesus had performed many miraculous works, which gave away the answer. What is so revealing about Jesus's reply, however, is the name by which he performs his works: "I did tell you and you don't believe. . . . The works that I do in my Father's name testify about me. But you don't believe because you are not of my sheep" (vv. 25–26). Because Jesus performs miracles in the name of the Father, the Jews should be able to see what is so lucid: unless Jesus is the Son who is from the Father, he cannot perform such works with such divine power and authority to begin with. But his Jewish opponents were slow to understand because they were not his sheep (see vv. 26–27). How can one identify Jesus's sheep? "My sheep hear my voice, I know them, and they follow me. I give them eternal life, and they will never perish. No one will snatch them out of my hand" (vv. 27–28). Now what assurance can Jesus offer his listeners that no one—not even the devil himself—can snatch his sheep out of his hand? Here is how Jesus answers: "My Father, who has given them to me, is greater than all. No one is able to snatch them out of the Father's hand. I and the Father are one" (vv. 29–30). Jesus's sheep lack no confidence that he will keep them from perishing because the Father is the one who first gave them to the Son, the same Father who is one with his Son.

Some subordinationists may try to wiggle their way out of John 10, as if Jesus merely means he is in sync with the will of the Father. However, if such a weak picture of unity were true, the Jews would not have reacted with such vitriol. "Again the Jews picked up rocks to stone him," said the apostle John (v. 31). Jesus responded, "I have shown you many good works from the Father. For which of these works are you stoning me?" (v. 32), to which the Jews answered, "We aren't stoning you for a good work . . . but for blasphemy, because you–being a man–make yourself God" (v. 33). However miscued their understanding of Jesus may have been, the Jews understood enough to hear his claim to be one with the Father and to conclude that it is blasphemy if not true. For Jesus was not claiming a mere unity of will(s) with his Father, but he was claiming a unity of essence—and his works proved as much. John 10 is a provocative narrative not despite simplicity but precisely because of simplicity. Jesus is claiming to subsist in the same, simple divine essence as the Father. Except for their personal properties, all that is in the Father is in the Son—no common property is withheld. For he is eternally begotten from the Father's divine essence.

Furthermore, when we speak of the Father begetting the Son, the riches of divine simplicity shower the Son's generation from all sides. The Arians could not accept a Son who is one with the

Father because they could not imagine a Son eternally begotten from the Father's nature, apart from a division of essence. To quote Athanasius, the Arians "deny that the Son is the proper offspring of the Father's essence, on the ground that this must imply parts and divisions."[20] A division of parts is no doubt present with human generation. A human father passes on part of his essence when he begets a son. But the Arians failed to consider whether such a human limitation should be imposed on divinity. A human father passes on a part of his substance, but God the Father communicates the entirety of the divine essence to his Son in generation. "The Father in begetting the Son did not pass on part of his nature to the Son, but bestowed the whole nature upon him," says Aquinas.[21] Begetting does not forfeit the simplicity of the Trinity because the Father begets his Son without division or partition.

If the Father eternally generates his Son without division, then the Son receives his generation from the Father without change as well. In our human experience, to receive something from someone else means the recipient is being acted on, even modified as a result—we are creatures who are subject to a passive potency. However, if the Father and the Son are pure act, then the eternal generation of the Son is no mutation. In that sense, eternal generation is not something that "happens" to the Son, but he *is* the only begotten Son, which is why we say his personal property *is* filiation. The "Son's begottenness is not the actualization of some passive potency in God, nor is it something that is 'done to' the

---

[20] Athanasius, *Against the Arians*, 1.5.15, (*NPNF* 4:315). To see all that we should preclude from eternal generation, consult Barrett, *Simply Trinity*, 166–175. Our section here elaborates on this work, which gives more attention to nine marks of what Barrett calls an "unhealthy generation."

[21] Aquinas, *Summa Theologiae*, 1a.39.3

Son. The Son just is the eternal generation from the Father," says Dolezal. "This is because God's simplicity pertains not merely to the divine substance, but to the divine persons as well."[22]

Simplicity cloaks the doctrine of eternal generation so that the Father drapes all the perfections of the divine essence—from eternity to immutability—over his Son, a pure act of generation that guarantees the Son's equality with the Father. The same logic applies when contemplating the eternal spiration of the Spirit from the Father and the Son.[23]

Challenges the Church Faces Today

As the church faces new and unique obstacles today, simplicity has never been more relevant. Over the last century modern theologians claimed to be experiencing a revival of the Trinity, but further investigation has revealed a different verdict: the Trinity they resuscitated was not the Trinity of classical Christianity, as articulated since the Nicene Creed. Instead, many used the vocabulary of the creed but substituted its true meaning for a *social* Trinity. Advocates of social trinitarianism are diverse, some more extreme than others, but certain characteristics define social trinitarianism nonetheless.[24]

---

[22] Dolezal, "Trinity," 92, 88. And again, "The Son and Spirit are not subjects to whom generation and spiration 'happen'; rather, they simply *are* the 'happening' of generation and spiration as considered under the relations of filiation and procession respectively." Dolezal, 91–92.

[23] If simplicity is true, then the eternal generation of the Son and the eternal spiration of the Spirit are not divisible acts either. To see why, consult Dolezal, "Trinity," 93.

[24] Examples of social trinitarians include: Jürgen Moltmann, Miroslav Volf, Leonardo Boff, etc. For the context of its rise to influence, see Barrett, *Simply Trinity*, 74–85.

Social trinitarians generally do not begin with the unity of the Trinity, and some are outright hostile to simplicity. For a variety of reasons, they believe we must begin with the plurality of the persons instead. Furthermore, *person* no longer means what it used to mean. For example, the great tradition defined a divine person as one who is "most perfect in the whole of nature, namely what subsists in rational nature." Or, to use our language of eternal relations of origin, a person is a "relation as subsisting in the divine nature."[25] The great tradition distinguished the persons but, as John Owen said, they always believed "a divine person is nothing but *the divine essence . . . subsisting in an especial manner*."[26] Such a conviction certified the persons had *all* things in common except their personal relations. Social trinitarianism, however, did not define the persons with simplicity in view. Their priority was to emphasize plurality, but not just any plurality. Beginning with the persons, social trinitarians concluded that each person is its own, separate center of consciousness and will. As a result, there is not one will according to the Trinity's one, simple essence (pro-Nicene trinitarianism), but there are three wills according to each person's individual, independent center of consciousness.

Social trinitarians redefined "relations" as well. The focus was no longer on the eternal relation of origin or the persons as subsisting relations of the same, simple divine essence. Instead, the focus shifted: the persons became a society of relationships between individuals with their independent volitions. The emphasis swung from ontology to functionality, from being to becoming. Mutuality, especially each person's social interaction with one another, took precedence. The emphasis now fell on the persons as autonomous,

---

[25] Aquinas, *Summa Theologiae*, 1a.29.3 and 1a.39.1.
[26] Owen, *Brief Vindication*, in *Works* 2:407; emphasis in the original.

volitional individuals within a divine society, each with its own will and, therefore, capable of interpersonal relationships with one another. Unity was no longer defined according to the Trinity's simplicity but explained by each person's mutual synergy or cooperation with one another within this divine society.

In addition, social trinitarians criticized the classical distinction between God in himself (*ad intra*) and God toward creation (*ad extra*). Nor were they content with the classical distinction between the Trinity's processions and missions. Rather, they collapsed these categories into one another. Such an instinct began with a theologian named Karl Rahner who said, "The 'economic' Trinity is the 'immanent' Trinity and the 'immanent' Trinity is the 'economic' Trinity."[27] Such a conflation was intentional and proved advantageous: if the Trinity is social—a society of separate centers of consciousness and will—these divine persons can be the model for human society, a society that also requires cooperation between persons with their own centers of consciousness and will. Thus began a quest for the proper paradigm between the Trinity and society. Social trinitarianism became the prototype for innumerable agendas, including politics, ecclesiology, and sexuality.

Unfortunately, evangelicals have been influenced by social trinitarianism in a variety of ways. First, it is no secret that evangelicals in the last century have abandoned the Trinity's simplicity, rejected classical distinctions between the persons such as eternal generation,

---

[27] Karl Rahner, *The Trinity* (New York: Crossroad, 1997), 22. Do notice, Rahner even changed the vocabulary to "immanent" and "economic." As Barrett explains throughout *Simply Trinity*, this is a shift away from the older vocabulary of "processions" and "missions." For a recent critique of Rahner, see Thomas Joseph White, *The Trinity: On the Nature and Mystery of the One God* (Washington, DC: Catholic University of America Press, 2022), 578–86.

and sometimes outright asserted three centers of consciousness and will.[28] Second, evangelicals have not only turned toward a social Trinity but, in doing so, they have also introduced societal hierarchy between the persons. Social trinitarians considered their social Trinity a model of equality between the persons and, by consequence, justification for equality in civil government, in church polity, and between the sexes. However, evangelicals used the vocabulary of a social Trinity to establish a functional hierarchy between the divine persons, a hierarchy that is the exemplar for hierarchy between the sexes.

For example, some evangelicals have advocated for the eternal functional subordination of the Son (EFS).[29] According to EFS, the Trinity is a type of society or community in which the persons are equal in essence but not in role. The Father has a greater authority and glory than the Son and the Spirit. For instance, the Son is called *Son* because he is functionally subordinate to his Father. Advocates of EFS now accept the eternal generation of the Son, but they have (mis)used this Nicene doctrine to further substantiate the Son's functional subordination to the Father from eternity. The Son's functional subordination is found within and even flows from his eternal generation from the Father. Unlike Nicaea, the Son is not *Son* due to his eternal generation alone, but his functional

---

[28] Examples are many, but consider J. P. Moreland and William Lane Craig, *Philosophical Foundations for a Christian Worldview*, 2nd ed. (Downers Grove, IL: IVP Academic, 2017), 583.

[29] For what follows, see Wayne Grudem, *Systematic Theology* (Grand Rapids: Zondervan Academic, 2022); Bruce Ware, *Father, Son, and Spirit: Relationships, Roles, and Relevance* (Wheaton, IL: Crossway, 2005); Bruce Ware, "Unity and Distinction of the Trinitarian Persons," in *Trinitarian Theology: Theological Models and Doctrinal Applications,* ed. Keith S. Whitfield (Nashville: B&H Academic, 2019), 17–62. For a much more thorough critique than what this chapter gives here, see Barrett, *Simply Trinity,* chap. 8.

subordination to the Father also makes him a Son. Therefore, the Son's eternal submission to the Father is the fitting prototype for the woman's submission to the man in marriage and society.

These new challenges are not merely entertained at the academic level but have pervaded evangelical churches for half a century. Measured responses have been written against social trinitarianism, including the EFS variety. But to recover biblical orthodoxy in the church, we must at least address the ways simplicity has been compromised.

First, divine simplicity and three centers of consciousness and will are antithetical, which explains why social trinitarians either desert simplicity altogether or attempt a revision that so softens simplicity that it does not conflict.

Second, there is good reason why social trinitarians have been occupied fending off accusations of tritheism. Once unity is no longer explained primarily by simplicity but by a cooperation of each person's separate, independent will, one must explain how three volitional faculties do not result in three essences. The burden of proof is on social trinitarians to demonstrate why the idea of three centers of consciousness does not result in three different, independent gods, for the persons are no longer subsisting relations of the same, simple essence *and will*.

Third, variations of social trinitarianism like EFS face a predicament: They deny that there are three wills in the Trinity, but how can one person be functionally subordinate and submit to another person within the immanent life of the Trinity without each person exercising its own will? In the great tradition, obedience was only possible for the Son by virtue of his incarnation. By assuming a human nature, he assumed everything that makes that nature human, a human will included. To say, as EFS does, that the Son *as Son* is functionally subordinate to his Father *ad intra*, as if such a role is a second personal property next to eternal generation, requires the Son to have his own, independent will. They can deny multiple wills in the Trinity, but the logical consequence of a subordinate Son cannot avoid it. Again, the burden of proof is on them to explain how they dodge tritheism.

Fourth, by inserting functional subordination within eternal generation, EFS must explain how such hierarchy does not surrender simplicity. EFS promises that the Son is only subordinate in role, not essence—in function, not substance. And they have now used eternal generation to further substantiate that claim, saying the Son's functional subordination is found within and flows from eternal generation. Such a maneuver seriously misunderstands the purpose of the Nicene Creed, however. Our church fathers did not put eternal generation forward to justify functional subordination but to accomplish the exact opposite purpose. Eternal generation was put forward to defend the total equality of the Son against Arians who considered the Son subordinate not only in essence but also in function—the Son only shares a unity in will(s) with the Father. Therefore, the church fathers were clear on two fronts: (1) eternal generation (and eternal generation alone) distinguishes the Son as *Son*; and (2) eternal generation is a key that locks any and all subordination out of the Trinity. For this reason, the pro-Nicene tradition has always defended the biblical teaching of the Son's coequality with the Father by appealing to the Son's generation from the Father's *essence*.[30] If functional subordination is to be located *within* eternal generation, then what is to keep subordination out of the essence

---

[30] Examples are legion (from the Cappadocian Fathers to Augustine, from Anselm to Aquinas, from Francis Turretin to John Owen). But see Athanasius, *Against the Arians* 1.9.29 (*NPNF*[2] 4:324); Athanasius, *Defense of the Nicene Definition* 5.19 (*NPNF*[2] 4:162–63).

when eternal generation, by definition, means the Son is begotten from the Father's *essence*? As we have emphasized, the persons *are* the divine essence, just subsisting in a special mode or manner. Richard Muller summarizes the orthodox position well: "There is . . . no real distinction between the three persons and the divine essence, as if the essence were one thing (*res*) and the three persons another thing, for God is a simple and noncomposite being."[31]

Fifth, Scripture never speaks of the Son as "less" than the Father except when the Son has taken on the "form of a servant" (Phil 2:7). Submission is not what makes him a Son. Obedience is so scandalous during the incarnation *because* obedience is not what the Son just "does anyway." The point of the incarnation is not to feature a Son who is already submissive apart from his mission in the world. Rather, the incarnation leaves us in shock because the Son left the glory of heaven to undergo the humiliation of crucifixion. "And being found in human form, he humbled himself by becoming obedient to the point of death, even death on a cross" (Phil 2:7–8 ESV). Hebrews accentuates the same contrast: "Although he was a son, he learned obedience through what he suffered" (5:8 ESV). To insert obedience into the Godhead—the Trinity *ad intra*—is to project something quite human into the divine. While EFS continues to insist that the Son is a lesser glory and authority than the Father, the Athanasian Creed says just the opposite: "The divinity of the Father, Son, and Holy Spirit is one, the glory equal, the majesty coeternal."[32]

---

[31] Richard A. Muller, *Post-Reformation Reformed Dogmatics* (Grand Rapids: Baker Academic, 2003), 4:191. He is quoted in Dolezal, who says it this way: the persons "are simply the divine essence subsisting in a threefold manner." "Trinity," 94.

[32] Van Dixhoorn, *Creeds*, 21. Notice the parallel to Jesus's words in John 5:22–23, which ascribe equal glory to the Son as to the Father. The

The External Works of the Trinity Are Undivided

When we contemplate every one of God's wondrous works, Scripture leaves us with one conclusion: the Father, Son, and Spirit work indivisibly in creation, providence, and salvation. They are not independent persons who operate each with his own will but who happen to cooperate with one another to bring about an agreed-upon plan. Rather, Father, Son, and Spirit perform every work according to their one, simple will. For every work is from the Father through the Son by the Spirit. The church fathers had a saying that encapsulated this biblical observation: "The external works of the Trinity are undivided."[33]

To contemplate the Trinity in the church means we cannot limit our vision to what God has done, but Scripture intends to lift our heads so that we gaze at who God is. As we are brought into contact with the inseparability of the persons in their external works, how can we not envisage the indivisibility of their essence? The unity of the Trinity in the economy of salvation is designed to draw our eyes heavenward until we are wonderstruck at the simplicity of the Trinity. In the words of Gregory of Nyssa, "As we say that the operation of the Father, and the Son, and the Holy Spirit is one, so we say that the Godhead is one."[34]

---

creed emphasizes the same when it says there are not three Almighties but one Almighty.

[33] Augustine is credited with this aphorism, translated from the Latin *opera trinitatis ad extra sunt indivisa*. See Bradley G. Greene, ed., *Shapers of Christian Orthodoxy* (Downers Grove, IL: IVP, 2010), 241. See chapter 6 in this volume for more on this.

[34] To consider his statement in context, see Gregory of Nyssa, *On the Holy Trinity* (*NPNF*² 5:326–30).

CHAPTER FOUR

The Son and His Father
Eternal Generation

J esus Christ is the cornerstone of the Christian religion. The Scripture speaks of him in majestic superlatives that invoke worship from those who seek to follow this carpenter from Nazareth. The Bible describes Jesus as the head of the church who is preeminent over all things (Col 1:18), the One who is much greater than angels (Heb 1:4), the One through whom all things were made and to whom all things will return (Rom 11:36), the One who is upholding the universe by the word of his power (Heb 1:3), the One who gave his life for the unrighteous that they might enjoy the riches of his righteousness (2 Cor 5:21); simply put, in the Christian life, Jesus is our all-in-all, our only hope in life and death.

It is for good reason, then, that the Christians spend their days contemplating this man Jesus Christ. Hebrews 12 starts off with the imperative to "consider him who endured such hostility from sinners against himself" (v. 3). This imperative to "consider him" is the rhythm of grace in which the Christian life finds beauty. When

Christians bend their minds toward Christ and "consider him," we are met with the true, the good, and the beautiful in the person and work of Jesus Christ. Considering Jesus brings our soul to the living water so that when we drink, we will no longer thirst (John 7:37). Christ is the well from which we must drink often.

As Christians, we seek to glorify the Lord with not just our strength and our soul but also our *minds* (Mark 12:30), so we ought to consider Jesus Christ, the Second Person of the Trinity. In considering and contemplating the Second Person of the Trinity, we will find an infinite impetus for worship. Our minds ought to tread down the variegated paths of consideration: for example, we ought to consider the life-changing truths of our union with Jesus; we ought to consider the glorious and gruesome atonement of Jesus; we ought to consider the victorious resurrection and ascension of Jesus. These moments in the unfolding economy of salvation ought to take up time and space in the thoughts of Christians.

We ought not just think about the *work* of Christ either, but also the *person* of Christ. As we think about notions like his life, death, and resurrection, those instances of Christ's work will be all the more illuminated when we realize that *this* man did *these* works. We ought to consider questions pertaining to Christ's *person*—questions such as, What does it mean for Jesus to be true man and true God at the same time? What does it mean for the incorporeal to experience life in space? What does it mean for the immutable to grow older each day? What does it mean for Jesus to simultaneously know all things and yet confess that he does not know "that day or hour" (Mark 13:32)?

This exercise—considering the person and work of Jesus Christ—has been the church's vocation since Peter's sermon in Acts 2. Since her conception, the church has wrestled with just who this person is and what exactly he has accomplished. This cosmic conversation concerning Christ has spanned characters, continents, and centuries. Much thought has passed, and ink been spilt, throughout the church's history on this man Jesus Christ.

We have already heard from one of the earliest trinitarian contests—the Council of Nicaea. The Son's eternal relation to the Father was the most significant point of contention at the council. On the one hand, the church wanted to protect the oneness of God, which is so indispensable to Christianity. For the Christian religion is a monotheistic religion that emphatically declares that "the LORD our God, the LORD is one" (Deut 6:4). On the other hand, the Christian religion emphasizes the coequality of three divine persons—the Father, the Son, and the Holy Spirit. The doctrinal tension became apparent in the third century as groups of Christian thinkers battled against one another concerning whether or not Jesus was of the *same* substance as the Father (what came to be known as *homoousios*, or in Greek, "of the same substance"), or if Jesus was of a *similar* substance to the Father (what came to be known as *homoiousios*, or in Greek, "of a similar substance").

Given these questions, the student seeking to study Christ will recognize that it is an impossibility to cast your mind toward Christ and not also contemplate the Father and the Son. While this book does not have an individual chapter covering that field of theology called *paterology* (the study of the Father), we will nevertheless consider the First Person of the Trinity—the Father—through this book and particularly in this chapter. As a first fruit demonstration, it would be a frustrating endeavor to consider what it means for Christ to be a *Son* without allowing your contemplation to lead toward what it means for the First Person of the Trinity to be a *Father*.

Returning to those vital questions arising out of the Council of Nicaea, issues concerning Jesus's eternal relation of origin are inevitable when considering this early church conversation.

Though there was much more going on in the Council of Nicaea than this individual question, this question gets at the heart of the discussion: If all things can be divided into the categories of Creator or creature, where should we put Jesus? Does Jesus deserve to be on the side of the Creator, on the side of him who brings all things about by the word of his power? Or on the contrary, should the church relegate Jesus to the side of creation, as one who was brought about? Exploring this question and its corollaries will take us to the doctrine of eternal generation. As those orthodox theologians who prevailed at the Council of Nicaea codified what would become the official teaching of the church catholic (small *c*, meaning "universal"), the doctrine of eternal generation became vital in explaining a mature understanding of Jesus Christ.

That is the aim of this chapter—to examine the doctrine of eternal generation for the sake of "rediscovering" the eternal generation of the Son for the church today. We will pursue this goal by arriving at a working definition of eternal generation. Next, we will turn to explicate the implication of the doctrine for the Christian life. We will hold up the doctrine, like a diamond, so we can see it shine. For not only does the doctrine of eternal generation give us a better understanding of the *person* of Jesus Christ, it will also help us better understand the *work* of Jesus as we make sense of his mission. So we will work to "define" the doctrine of eternal generation and then "declare" the doctrine of eternal generation.

If you have never before heard of eternal generation, you will meet a historic doctrine that has been affirmed by Christians throughout the centuries. But whether you are unfamiliar with the doctrine or you already bring some awareness to the reading, our hope is that this doctrine becomes a *living* doctrine. Eternal generation is not merely an isolated doctrine that stays in the realm of ontological theory alone, but instead it is a doctrine to be treasured, as it both instructs us about the person of our Savior and bears significant importance in the Christian life.

What Is Eternal Generation?

In its most simple form, the doctrine of eternal generation is a Christian doctrine that attempts to articulate how the Bible describes Jesus as being *from* the Father. John Webster writes of the doctrine, "Eternal generation is the personal and eternal act of God the Father whereby he is the origin of the personal subsistence of God the Son, so communicating to the Son the one undivided divine essence."[1] While we will come to see the nuances of this definition in due time, it is vital for readers to see at least two aspects of the doctrine: First, eternal generation gets at the Son's eternal relation of origin *from* the Father. This "from-ness" is an eternal "from-ness" without the stamp of time or chronology. Jesus is ever from the Father. Second, in the eternal generation of the Son, the Father communicates the "undivided divine essence" to the Son such that whatever the Father is, the Son is likewise. We

---

[1] John Webster, "Eternal Generation," in *God Without Measure: Working Papers in Christian Theology*, vol. 1, *God and the Works of God* (London: T&T Clark, 2018), 1:30. Others have defined eternal generation similarly. For example, see Benedict Pictet, who defined the doctrine saying, "This generation no mortal can comprehend; in fact we do not understand by the term anything else, than that the Father from all eternity shared his name, his perfections, and his glory, with the Son." Pictet, *Christian Theology*, trans. Frederick Reyroux (London: Seeley and Sons, 1834), 113. Also see Matthew Barrett, who defines the doctrine, "From all eternity, the Father communicates the one, simple, undivided divine essence to the Son." Matthew Barrett, *Simply Trinity: The Unmanipulated Father, Son, and Spirit* (Grand Rapids: Baker, 2021), 161.

will come back to these two truths when we look at the church's codified belief in the doctrine of eternal generation. For now, this framework will allow us to explore the doctrine a bit further, starting with the biblical data.

While the point of this chapter is to contemplate the doctrine of eternal generation and why eternal generation as both a biblical and historical doctrine has meaning in the life of the church, it is also important to keep a robust paterology together with our Christology. Insomuch as the doctrine of eternal generation can be said to be Jesus's eternal relation of origin to the Father (meaning, the doctrine of eternal generation attempts to describe Jesus's being *from* the Father), we cannot separate conversations about the Father from conversations about the Son. Neither should we want to do so or try to do so. For the Father is that person of the Trinity who is the principle and source of all things. The Father alone dwells in the personal property of "unbegottenness." As we saw in the chapter on the Trinity and the doctrine of simplicity, the fact that the three persons of the Trinity are the same essence (*homoousia*) makes them *one*, and yet the Christian doctrine of the eternal relations of origin demonstrates how, while they are truly one, they are nevertheless *three*. So throughout the centuries of the Christian church, the maxim has been *"One God, three persons"*—*one* in essence but distinguishable by the reality that the Father is unbegotten and the principle and source of all things; the Son is eternally begotten from the Father's simple undivided essence, and the Spirit proceeds eternally from both the Father and the Son.

With these needed caveats in place, we can now turn to further explore the focus of this chapter in particular—the biblical notion of Jesus being eternally from the Father by that doctrine the church has called *eternal generation*.

Eternal Generation in Scripture

The biblical data is far too comprehensive to convey in one chapter, but since Scripture is the rule and norm of the church, it is too vital to gloss over.[2] In this section, we simply show a threefold method for demonstrating the doctrine of eternal generation from Scripture. We can see the doctrine when bringing biblical and theological reasoning together and considering (1) those texts which describe the Son as "begotten," (2) those texts which describe Jesus as the "Son of God," and (3) those moments in the unfolding drama of Scripture that attest to the eternal processions not only by way of content but also by way of revelation and the shape of the canon.

When these considerations are taken together, careful readers of Scripture will see that the doctrine of eternal generation relies on more than merely a few scattered verses. Although there is no verse that presents a mature understanding of the doctrine in all its nuance and complexity, when we bring together the variegated biblical data and seek to make sense of it, a robust doctrine of eternal generation will emerge. Therefore, the doctrine of eternal generation will not only make sense of a few scattered verses but also enable the church to make sense of Jesus's relationship to the Father in the whole of Scripture.

---

[2] For a more complete treatment of the biblical data, see Kevin Giles, *The Eternal Generation of the Son: Maintaining Orthodoxy in Trinitarian Theology* (Downers Grove: IVP Academic, 2012), 63–91. See also the essays from Scott R. Swain, Matthew Y. Emerson, Mark S. Gignilliat, D. A. Carson, Charles Lee Irons, Madison N. Pierce, and R. Kendall Soulen in Fred Sanders and Scott R. Swain, *Retrieving Eternal Generation* (Grand Rapids: Zondervan, 2017), 29–149. Finally, see also, Petrus van Mastricht, *Theoretical-Practical Theology*, vol. 2, *Faith in the Triune God*, ed. Joel R. Beeke (Grand Rapids: Reformation Heritage, 2019), 546–62.

First, there is the biblical notion of Jesus's being "begotten" by the Father. The notion of "begottenness" can be found in texts such as Ps 2:7; Prov 8:25; Acts 13:33; and Heb 1:5.[3] Maybe the most well-known of all the "begotten" texts is John 3:16.[4] To make sense of the "begotten" language, we should also consider those texts that establish Jesus's familial title of *Son*.

Second, there are variegated pericopes and passages to which we could turn in developing the sonship of Jesus Christ. Far from being a mere throwaway title that can be read over throughout the Bible, the term *Son*, when used of Jesus Christ, has significant meaning for our trinitarianism. Consider John 8, for example. In this chapter, Jesus is quarreling with the Pharisees about his identity. At one point, the Pharisees directly ask Jesus, "Who are you?" (v. 25), and Jesus answers them with a certain level of vagueness that comes as a condemnation. Jesus answers them by directing the conversation to the "one who sent me." (v. 26) This answer does not go over well with the Pharisees, who claim their authority comes from none other than Abraham (v. 33). Although this is an impressive lineage to be sure, Jesus takes his claim a step further and claims that though

---

[3] Of course, it should be noted that the two Old Testament references, along with their New Testament quotations, are debated concerning their relation to eternal generation. See, for example, D. Glenn Butner Jr.'s discussion of these passages and two separate hermeneutical options on understanding them: D. Glenn Butner Jr., *Trinitarian Dogmatics: Exploring the Grammar of the Christian Doctrine of God* (Grand Rapids: Baker Academic, 2022), 64–66. Moreover, the Emerson and Pierce essays in Sanders and Swain, eds., *Retrieving Eternal Generation*, tackle the exegetical questions of Proverbs 8 and Hebrews 1, respectively.

[4] There is disagreement over how *monogenēs* ought to be translated. For a defense of "only begotten" instead of "unique" or "one and only," see Charles Lee Irons, "A Lexical Defense of the Johannine 'Only Begotten'" in Sanders and Swain, eds., *Retrieval Eternal Generation*, 98–116.

they think they are from Abraham, their actual father is the devil. They do not understand him because they come from their "father" the devil, but he comes from the Father himself. Jesus says, "If God were your Father, you would love me, because I came from God and I am here. For I didn't come on my own, but he sent me" (v. 42). Jesus's claim here is rather startling: while Jesus is the Son of God the Father, the Pharisees are sons of the devil. Therefore, they do not have eyes to see and ears to hear that if Jesus has been sent by the Father, he must be eternally begotten from the Father.

Beyond the significant claims of John 8, readers could turn as well to Matt 3:17; 11:27; 17:5; 24:36–39; Mark 1:11; 3:11; 9:7; Luke 4:41; 8:28; John 1:14; 5:19; 5:26; Heb 1:5; 2 Pet 1:17; 1 John 4:10; and more. These passages come together and should act as a loud siren to the reader: there is meaning in that title—*Son*. For those who spend much time in the Scriptures and who have a familiarity with the biblical narrative, it might be easy to read over the Christological title of *Son* when Jesus is referred to as the "Son of God." Yet we might remind ourselves of what both Augustine and Petrus van Mastricht have taught with clarity—the familial titles within the Godhead bear significance, and it is for good reason that the Scriptures do not simply refer to the persons of the Trinity as "three brothers."[5] Indeed, the triune persons are *not* three brothers, nor three cousins, nor three social relationships. Instead, the biblical language of "Father," "Son," and "Spirit" says something intentional and meaningful about their eternal relations.

---

[5] See Augustine, *De Trinitate*, ed. John E. Rotelle OSA and Edmund Hill OP, 2nd ed. (Hyde Park, NY: New City, 2012), 27.50; and Mastricht, *Theoretical-Practical Theology*, 2:557–58.

D. A. Carson writes, "'Son' language tied to 'Father' language is one of the unavoidable hints that the relationship between the 'Father' and the 'Son' is rightly conceived of in terms of generation—indeed, of eternal generation."[6] The Second Person of the Trinity—Jesus Christ—is called a "Son" for a strikingly simple reason: he really *is* a Son. The Second Person of the Trinity really is a Son to the First Person of the Trinity, who really is a Father to the Second Person of the Trinity. The familiar titles of *Father* and *Son* are not accidental but quite meaningful. As Jesus is called "The Son of Man" because he is born of Mary, he is called "The Son of God" because he is eternally generated (or begotten) by the Father.[7] The doctrine of eternal generation will help the church properly order and describe how we are to think of this sonship of Jesus.

Third, as mentioned in chapter 2, there is something of a revelation of eternal processions—including eternal generation—in not just the text of Scripture but the *shape* of Scripture as well. This is why Fred Sanders can say, "The revelation of the Trinity occurred primarily in the historical event of the arrival of the persons of the Son and the Holy Spirit."[8] A glorious truth about the Christian Scripture is that we not only see the Trinity through exegetical attentiveness to the actual content and words of Scripture, but we also see the triune God in examining those moments within God's economy that give shape to the Scripture. For example, consider *when* we learn of each person of the Trinity. We learn of the Father in the opening salvo of Scripture as the drama inaugurates saying,

---

[6] D. A. Carson, "John 5:26: *Crux Interpretum* for Eternal Generation," in Sanders and Swain, *Retrieving Eternal Generation*, 87.

[7] We recognize that sometimes "Son of Man" can also have other meanings, both messianic and divine.

[8] Fred Sanders, *The Triune God* (Grand Rapids: Zondervan, 2016), 124.

"In the beginning God . . ." (Gen 1:1). We learn there is a Son and Second Person of the Trinity as the new covenant tells us, "In the beginning was the Word, and the Word was with God, and the Word *was* God" (John 1:1; emphasis added). We learn there is a Spirit and Third Person of the Trinity as Peter begins to preach to the people who would become the Church of Jerusalem and as the Spirit descends at Pentecost (Acts 2:1–4). To summarize this third method Sanders writes:

> In order to inform us that the Father has a Son and a Holy Spirit, the Father sent the Son and the Holy Spirit in person. The triunity of God was revealed when the persons of the Trinity became present among us in a new way, showing up in person and becoming the object of our human observation. . . . In the fullness of time, God did not give us facts about himself, but gave us himself in the person of the Father who sent, the Son who was sent, and the Holy Spirit who was poured out. These events were accompanied by verbally inspired explanatory words; but the latter depend on the former.[9]

Missions Are Fitting with the Trinity's Eternal Relations of Origin		
Person	**Eternal Relation**	**Economic Event**
Father	Paternity	Creation
Son	Filiation	Incarnation
Spirit	Spiration	Pentecost

---

[9] Sanders, 40.

Begotten, Not Made

Now that we have established the doctrine of eternal generation as a thoroughly biblical doctrine, we can proceed to develop the nuances needed for a well-rounded understanding of the doctrine. To do so, we must bring our collective attention back to what was called previously in this book, "our heritage"—the Nicene Creed. When the Nicene Creed begins to describe Jesus Christ in lines 3–7, it is important to notice that the creed states that he is (1) begotten, not made, and (2) of one substance with the Father:

> I believe in one God, the Father Almighty,
> Maker of heaven and earth, and of all things visible and invisible.
> And in one Lord Jesus Christ, the only-begotten Son of God,
> begotten of the Father before all worlds;
> God of God, Light of Light, very God of very God;
> begotten, not made, being of one substance with the Father,
> by whom all things were made. . . .
> And I believe in the Holy Spirit, the Lord and Giver of life;
> who proceeds from the Father and the Son;
> who with the Father and the Son together is worshiped and glorified.[10]

In one way, the pedagogy behind eternal generation is rather "built in," as each of us knows what it means to be generated. Each living person today has been "generated" from his or her biological father and mother and in this way can relate to the notion of generation. However, as mentioned in chapter 1, your

---

[10] Chad Van Dixhoorn, *Creeds, Confessions, and Catechisms: A Reader's Edition* (Wheaton, IL: Crossway, 2022), 17–18.

generation and the eternal generation of the Son are quite different for at least two reasons.

The first difference is that your generation has a time stamp. There was a time before your generation and there is a time after your generation. At one point in time and space, you were not, and then you began to be. This is not the case for the Son's generation, as his generation is an *eternal* generation in which the Father ever communicates the one divine substance to the Son. As seventh-century theologian John of Damascus wrote, "So then in the first sense of the word the three absolutely divine subsistences of the Holy Godhead agree: for they exist as one in essence. . . . For the Father alone is ingenerate, no other subsistence having given him being. And the Son alone is generate, for he was begotten of the Father's essence without beginning and without time."[11] For this reason, the Nicene Creed emphasizes that Jesus is *begotten*, not made. Jesus is eternally begotten, or eternally generated, from the Father; he is not a creation *of* the Father. The creed doubles down in this respect, noting that Jesus is the one "by whom all things were made." It is hard to exaggerate the importance of this distinction: if we can separate all things which have ever existed into the categories of *Creator* and *creature*, the Christian tradition has emphasized that Jesus belongs in the first category of *Creator*. Contrary to the teachings of Arius and those like him, there was never a time when Jesus was not. He is the eternally begotten Son who is the same yesterday, today, and forevermore (Heb 13:8).

The second difference between your generation and the Son's generation is that in your generation, you receive similar traits to your parents given that you share similar DNA. However, whereas you merely receive some *traits* of your biological parents, what

---

[11] John of Damascus, *Exposition of the Orthodox Faith* (*NPNF*[1] 9.9).

is communicated in the eternal generation of Jesus is the divine essence itself. So it is not the case that the Son merely receives *some* of the divine substance and shares in *some* of the divine perfection. Rather, the Father communicates the divine essence in its fullness to his Son in eternal generation. The Son *is* the divine essence. For the Son wholly and eternally subsists in the divine essence. Church history, as seen in the Nicene Creed, uses two important words to get at this reality: consubstantial and *homoousios*, or "of the same substance." We can see the emphasis of these two words in the Nicene articulation as the creed says that the Son is "of one substance with the Father." It would be incorrect to think of the Son as merely having enough attributes to be technically considered divine. On the contrary, Jesus doesn't merely have enough of the divine attributes to tip the scales towards divinity; rather, *whatever* the Father is the Son is likewise—save the *personal* designation of "unbegotten." As the Father is unchanging, the Son is unchanging; as "the Father has life in himself, so he has granted the Son also to have life in himself" (John 5:26 ESV); as the Father is omnipresent, the Son is omnipresent; as the Father is omnipotent, the Son is omnipotent. This pattern could be repeated for anything properly predicated of divinity.

As we learn from those who have gone before us, it will prove helpful to return again to John of Damascus, who helps illustrate both significant points here concerning the Son's eternal generation from the Father. John of Damascus wrote something of a summary of the Christian faith through a biblical and theological treatise called *An Exposition of the Orthodox Faith*. This particular work enjoys the chronological benefit of being at the end of what church historians call the Patristic Era. This means that John of Damascus was able to conduct his trinitarian theology with the major creeds and confessions of the church in his mind. He begins this work with a strong affirmation of God's incomprehensibility, which means we finite creatures can never circumscribe the Infinite One. After setting the stage with divine incomprehensibility, John of Damascus moves on to contemplating the Trinity through an affirmation and exposition of the Nicene Creed. His section on eternal generation is worth quoting in full:

> When we say that [Jesus] is before all ages, we mean that His begetting is outside of time and without beginning, for the Son of God was not brought from nothing into being; who is the brightness of the glory and the figure of the substance of the Father, His living power and wisdom, the subsistent Word, the substantial and perfect and living image of the invisible God. Actually, He was always with the Father, being begotten of Him eternally and without beginning. For the Father never was when the Son was not, but the Father and the Son begotten of Him exist together simultaneously, because the Father could not be so called without a Son.[12]

This quote is quite helpful, showcasing the significance of eternal generation. John of Damascus helps us see these important truths: (1) There was never a time "when the Son was not," as we have seen the ancient heretical group, the Arians, liked to say. Rather, the Son's generation, unlike your generation, is not confined by time but is *eternal*. (2) The doctrine of eternal generation makes

---

[12] John of Damascus, *The Orthodox Faith,* in *The Fathers of the Church,* vol. 37, trans. Frederic H. Chase Jr. (Washington, DC: Catholic University of America Press, 1958), 178.

sense of the familial language of "Father" and "Son." Some might worry that a notion of generation would make the Son "dependent" on the Father in a way that would lead to essential or functional subordination in eternity. This is not the case; in fact, as John of Damascus shows us, the Father could not be a father without the Son, just as the Son could not be a son without the Father. The Father's "unbegottenness" and the Son's eternal generation preserve the unity of essence between both. There is no subordination among a simple Trinity (see chapter 3). (3) The Son is *begotten, not made*. Here is the difference between orthodoxy and heresy, the latter putting one outside the fold of Christianity. The Son is not a created being. Rather, he is begotten of the very substance of the Father, not the product of a unique and individual *new* substance. Listen to the seventh-century theologian once more: "Begetting means producing of the substance of the begetter an offspring similar in substance to the begetter. Creation, on the other hand—making—is the bringing into being, from the outside and not from the substance of the creator, of something created and made entirely dissimilar [in substance]."[13]

To conclude this section, the doctrine of eternal generation is a doctrine which the church has long affirmed because it articulates the way in which the Scriptures speak about the Son's eternal relation to the Father. That relation is one in which the unbegotten Father eternally communicates the "one, simple, and undivided essence" to the Son. Therefore, the church can rightly confess, together with the Scriptures and the creeds that seek to faithfully summarize them, that Jesus is true God from true God, Light from Light, begotten, not made, and consubstantial with the Father.

---

[13] John of Damascus, *The Orthodox Faith*, 178–79.

Declaring the Doctrine of Eternal Generation

Now that we have arrived at a working definition and explored a few nuances of the doctrine of eternal generation, it is time to demonstrate the vitality of the doctrine in the life of the local church. In a sense, the doctrine of eternal generation enhances the Christian life in two important ways—what could be called "protective" and "provisional" applications. On the one hand, the doctrine of eternal generation will "protect" the church from faulty articulations both of the Trinity in general and of Christ in particular. Moreover, the doctrine of eternal generation also "provides" in the Christian life by ensuring that Jesus is the One uniquely qualified to save and redeem his people, the only One capable of resolving our God-sized problem. The rest of this chapter will explore these lanes of thinking: first, we will examine how the doctrine of eternal generation "protects" the church from faulty articulations of the Trinity and of Christology, and then we will conclude the chapter by showing how the doctrine of eternal generation "provides" the church with a healthy and glorious view of Jesus, who is uniquely capable of saving a wayward people. In the end, the doctrine of eternal generation ought to be seen as beautiful and true as it protects and provides for God's people—the church.

Eternal Generation as Protection

As for protecting the church's doctrine of the Trinity and a proper Christology, the doctrine of eternal generation demonstrates both the *unity* and *distinction* within the Godhead. Because of the doctrine of eternal generation, the church can be confident that Jesus is Lord, just as the Scripture proclaims. When Jesus proclaims that he and the Father are one (John 10:30), we can take his words with the upmost seriousness, knowing that the Father communicates the divine essence to the Son in eternal generation. In this way, a doctrine like eternal generation becomes an aid in more fruitful and appropriate Bible reading. As the creed says, articulating the biblical teaching, the Son is "of one substance with the Father." The First and Second Persons of the Trinity—Father and Son—are *homoousios*. That is, they are of the same substance. At the same time, the Father is not the Son, and the Son is not the Father. As the Nicene Creed answers the question, "How are the Father and the Son the same?" the creed is also equipped to answer the question, "How are the Father and the Son distinct?" Whereas the answer to the first question is the doctrine of *homoousios*, the answer to the second question is the doctrine of eternal generation and the distinction between paternity and filiation.

The Father is unbegotten and therefore the source or principle from which the Son and Spirit proceed. However, the Son is eternally generated by the Father. This distinction, which designates the Son's eternal relation of origin, is the *only* distinction we ought to make to differentiate the person of the Son from the Father. Of course, the distinction between the unbegotten Father and the eternally begotten Son will have implications for the works appropriated to each person within the divine economy (as we saw in the previous chapter). Nevertheless, eternal generation is the only thing which can be said to properly distinguish the Son from the Father. Having this biblical and creedal confession in mind will protect the church from a myriad of false trinitarian and Christological teachings.

If someone were to insist that the church ought to believe that "there was a time when the Son was not," the church ought to hold fast to her confession and declare that the Son is one with the Father and is eternally begotten from the Father. If someone were to insist that the church ought to believe that what actually distinguishes the persons of the Godhead is some *role* they perform or some authority they exercise, the church ought to hold fast to her confession and declare that eternal relations of origin alone distinguish the persons. If someone were to insist that the Son is of a lesser glory than the Father because the Father generates the Son, the church ought to hold fast to her confession and declare that far from eternal generation leading to a lesser glory, the doctrine, on the contrary, is what protects an equal glory. In the spirit of Nicaea, the Father eternally communicates the divine essence to the Son—the same essence the Father is, in all its glory.

Having a robust doctrine of eternal generation can protect the church in these and many more ways. Whether it be from formal heresies such as Arianism, Socinianism, and Adoptionism or from modern, novel misteaching about the Trinity, such as eternal functional subordination (EFS, also called "eternal relations of authority and submission"), the doctrine of eternal generation will protect the church's fidelity to her biblical confession.[14] Healthy guardrails in the life of the church are vital to maintaining confessional, orthodox fidelity. Having Scripture as our final authority and the church's long-held creeds as summative of Scripture, codified ecclesial doctrines like eternal generation come together to *protect* the church's witness about our Lord Jesus Christ

---

[14] Eternal functional subordination has been taught by theologians such as Wayne Grudem and Bruce Ware. For a critical response, see D. Glenn Butner Jr., *The Son Who Learned Obedience: A Theological Case against the Eternal Submission of the Son* (Eugene, OR: Pickwick, 2018), Barrett, *Simply Trinity,* 213–61; as well as Michael F. Bird and Scott Harrower, *Trinity Without Hierarchy: Reclaiming Nicene Orthodoxy in Evangelical Theology* (Grand Rapids: Kregel Academic, 2019).

and keep us from wandering from a proper confession about the cornerstone of the church.[15]

Finally, the doctrine of eternal generation protects the church by reminding us of what it means for Jesus to be a *Son*. Consider the example of the prodigal son recorded in Luke 15. In the parable, a man has two sons, and the younger son demands to receive his inheritance early so that he might spend it immediately. We read in the parable that the younger son spends his father's provisions unwisely. In fact, Luke tells us that the younger son's situation is so bad that at one point he "was longing to be fed with the pods that the pigs ate, and no one gave him anything" (v. 16 ESV). However, the glory of the story comes when this prodigal son decides to return home. On his journey homeward, he practices what he is going to say to his father, and he thinks to himself, "How many of my father's hired workers have more than enough food, and here I am dying of hunger! I'll get up, go to my father, and say to him, 'Father, I have sinned against heaven and in your sight. I'm no longer worthy to be called your son. Make me like one of your hired workers'" (vv. 17–19). Those who are familiar with the story know that when the father sees his son returning home, instead of chiding him for his disobedience, he runs to him and says, "My son is home" (v. 24, paraphrased). The prodigal son was ready to relinquish the title of "son" because he thought his disobedience disqualified him from such a title. Yet the father in the parable knows what any good father knows: regardless of what our children do—good or bad—they will always be *our* children.

---

[15] Building off three theologians—Gregory of Nyssa, Francis Turretin, and John Gill, Matthew Barrett lists nine ways the doctrine of eternal generation can be compromised: division of nature, multiplication of essence, priority or posteriority, motion, mutation, alteration, corruption, diminution, and cessation from operation. Barrett, *Simply Trinity*, 166–76.

The lesson of sonship in the parable is important because it is not our obedience or disobedience that defines our sonship or daughterhood. Rather, we are the sons or daughters of our parents because they *begot* us. No action will change this paternal relationship, whether from the child or the parent. What might this have to do with the doctrine of eternal generation? If we consider a major modern revision of classical trinitarianism like eternal functional subordination, as mentioned earlier, there are those who are tempted to define Jesus's personhood by his *obedience* or *submission* to the Father's authority. Yet this does a disservice to what it means to be a person and, even more important, to what it means to be a son. What makes Jesus the Son of God is not that he has been eternally submissive to the Father's will (as if they had different wills to begin with, which would divide the Trinity). Rather, what makes Jesus the Son of God is that he was *begotten* by the Father, and this is what makes *any* son a son of his father. Like human children, we do not define Jesus's sonship by any sort of authority or submission, but "begottenness." While the Scriptures do portray Jesus as obedient to the Father, this is an incarnational obedience that is only possible by means of his *humanity*. For the Son to be *eternally* obedient to the Father, it would require the Son to have an eternally separate will from the Father, which we said in chapter 3 cannot be the case, lest the simplicity of the Trinity be compromised. For this reason, and more, the church should choose her biblical and confessional inheritance over any modern revisions to what makes the Son—Jesus Christ—a son.

Eternal Generation as Provision

Not only does the doctrine of eternal generation *protect* the church from false articulations of Christ and the Trinity, but there are also proactive applications for the Christian life springing from the doctrine of eternal generation. In this way, the doctrine of eternal generation can be seen as provision in the Christian life. For in the doctrine of eternal generation the Christian can find a well of beauty and an anchor of salvific security. In this section, we will briefly explore (1) how the doctrine of eternal generation helps us understand more fully God's work in the economy of redemption and (2) how the doctrine of eternal generation answers one of humankind's biggest plights.

Christians can see the marvel and consistency between *who* God is and *what* God has done as they start to bring together the doctrine of eternal generation and God's marvelous work in redemption. While the works of God are not what distinguish between persons of the Trinity (for only the eternal relations of origin can do that), nevertheless, the careful student of God's work and Word will see that the *missions* of the Trinity fit the *processions* of the Trinity. As God the Father is unbegotten and eternally generates the perfect Son, it is God the Father who *sends* God the Son in the work of redemption. Jesus says in John 6:38 that he has come not to do his own will but the will of him who sent him. The Father sends the Son to complete the work of salvation, and this economic activity of the One who sends and the One who is sent is fitting in view of the One who generates and the One who is generated. We can see that "missions reflect and reveals the eternal relations of origin."[16] Far from having no meaningful import into the Christian life, the doctrine of eternal generation colors and gives a bit of ontological context to God's glorious work in the economy.

It is worth repeating that we do not reverse this order. We do not read the economic work of the triune God back *into* the

---

[16] This phrase comes from Barrett, *Simply Trinity*, 118.

persons of the Trinity, as if what the persons do in the economy constitutes who they are in their inner life. Rather, we read the fitting correspondence between processions and missions in *that* order—the persons of the Trinity inform the works of the Trinity. This is the proper, fitting material order of Christian theology: God first and then (and only by derivation) all things in relation to God. Christians will run into variegated theological issues if they try to take the work that God accomplishes among us creatures as definitional of the persons—even as that which constitutes the persons. So rather than the work determining categories of personhood in the Trinity, we confess that it is the processions that inform the missions. All the while, we hold in tension that it is most fundamentally *through* the works of the Trinity that we learn about the persons. However, this knowledge becomes chastened by the biblical data as the economy teaches about the persons and the persons dictate the economy. In this way, the Christian will always be a student, and worshipper, of the Trinity. The Christian will never graduate from the school of the Trinity. Rather, the pedagogy learned at the feet of the triune God is the kind of lesson that demands we go "further up" and "further in" as we ever participate in the grace and wonder that is our triune God.[17]

There will be more said about the relationship between the processions and missions later in this book when we explore the doctrine of inseparable operations. Yet it will be helpful here to note that, as

---

[17] This is, of course, a reference to that famous scene in Lewis's *Last Battle*, in which the numerous characters, finally experiencing the true Narnia, exclaim for the cast to progress "further up" and "further in": "I have come home at last! This is my real country! I belong here. This is the land I have been looking for all my life, though I never knew it till now. . . . Come further up, come further in." C. S. Lewis, *The Chronicles of Narnia: The Last Battle* (New York: Harper Collins, 1984), 213.

the doctrine of eternal generation helps Christians understand *both* the unity of the Trinity and the distinctions of the trinitarian persons, it will likewise make sense of the action of the Trinity. Scott Swain helpfully explores the unity of divine action. Swain writes, "All of God's external works are indivisible works of the one God: guided by God's singular divine wisdom, expressive of God's singular divine goodness, performed by God's singular divine power, aimed at God's singular divine glory."[18] While the Trinity acts as one, given that there is only one divine essence and therefore only one divine will, nevertheless, that action is appropriated in a way that fits each person's mode of subsistence. Swain continues this theme, saying, "As the Father's distinct personal mode of existing is to exist from no one but to beget the Son and breathe the Spirit, so the Father's distinct personal mode of acting is to act from no one but to act through the Son and by the Spirit." Swain continues, "As the Son's distinct personal mode of existing is to exist from the Father as his only begotten and to breathe the Spirit, so the Son's distinct personal mode of acting is to act from the Father and by the Spirit." Swain then moves to consider the Spirit's eternal relation of origin, "As the Spirit's distinct personal mode of existing is to be eternally breathed forth by the Father and the Son as the crowning procession of the Trinity, so his distinctive personal mode of acting is to act from the Father and the Son, bringing all of God's undivided external operations to their crowning fulfillment." In conclusion, "The one God's distinct personal modes of existing as Father, Son, and Spirit are inflected in the trinitarian shape of God's indivisible action: God's external actions proceed from the Father, through the Son, in the Spirit."[19]

---

[18] Scott R. Swain, *The Trinity: An Introduction* (Wheaton, IL: Crossway, 2020, 109.

[19] Swain, 109–10.

The trinitarian pedagogical loop, in which we learn about eternal generation from the mission of Jesus Christ and learn about the mission of Jesus Christ from eternal generation, eliminates notions of eternal generation not being a doctrine for the church. This doctrine deserves a pride of place within the life of God's people, for as we contemplate the Son's eternal generation *from* the Father, the church's doctrine of salvation will be rooted in the sturdiest of foundations—God himself.

Finally, not only does the doctrine of eternal generation color and contextualize the redemptive mission of the Son who redeems an unworthy people, the doctrine of eternal generation also establishes Jesus's unique identity as the only One qualified to redeem an unworthy people. In the simplest terms: as the deepest plight for humankind is sin and as sin is cosmic treason against a holy God, humankind has a God-sized problem that is simply out of our jurisdiction to fix.

Christian redemption is grander than the story of *bad* people becoming *good*. Christian salvation speaks a better word and presents before us a grand story of those who were *dead* becoming *alive*. As Paul's epistle to the church in Ephesus makes clear, we were a people who were dead in our sins (Eph 2:1). The sin that entangled humankind was more than a few wrongdoings and misgivings. Rather, a biblical understanding of sin brings forward the gravity of death. We were dead in our sins, unable to do good before the Lord, unable to provide the kind of atonement for our treason that would bring us back into right standing before a holy God. The good news of the Christian story is that while we lacked everything and had nothing to give, he who lacked nothing gave everything. The Lord saw our helpless estate and, like the good Father he is, did something about it. Because our sin was not a mere stain on our being but treason against the God of the cosmos, it was going to take none other than God to solve our God-sized problem.

This is where the doctrine of eternal generation enters the picture. Given what we have said thus far in this chapter about the eternal generation of Jesus, the Second Person of the Trinity is God. Jesus is God the Son, who is eternally generated by the Father. While this generation is eternal and a communication of the very divine essence, Jesus undertook another generation. This second generation is only an analogy of the first, for this second generation is the generation of Jesus's human nature and flesh from the woman Mary by the power of the Holy Spirit. While Jesus was eternally generated by the Father and therefore is divine, the human nature of Jesus was temporally generated by Mary. As that eternally begotten Son who is consubstantial with the Father and who now assumes a human flesh and body, Jesus can uniquely represent us before a holy God, yet he possesses the human nature that makes it possible for him to die on a Roman cross. Through his eternal generation, which is the explanation of his divinity, and his temporal generation, which is the explanation of his humanity, Jesus has the unique identity needed to reconcile God and man. At one time, Jesus Christ of Nazareth is both consubstantial (of the same substance) with the Father in his divinity and consubstantial with us in his humanity. Without the doctrine of eternal generation, we creatures would still be in our helpless estate, unable to remedy our God-sized problem.

While the Nicene Creed has received much deserved attention throughout this book, the Chalcedonian Creed (roughly AD 451) serves us well here as the creed that reminds us of this double generation. Chalcedon says that Christ was "begotten before all ages from the Father as regards his divinity, and in the last days the same for us and for our salvation from Mary, the Virgin God-bearer, as regards his humanity; one and the same Christ, Son, Lord, only-begotten, acknowledged in two natures which undergo no confusion, no change, no division, no separation." Christ was begotten from the Father "before the ages" and was begotten of Mary "in the last days."[20] The Son's eternal generation from the Father's divine nature and the temporal generation of the human nature from Mary is what makes Christ uniquely qualified to restore fellowship between God and humanity.

We need the Son to have the same substance as the Father that he might be our once and for all sacrifice (Heb 10:11–14). We need the Son to have the same substance as the Father that he might propitiate the wrath of our holy and just God (Rom 3:24–25). We need the Son to have the same substance as the Father that he might forever plead our case before God and not be prevented by death from continuing his priestly office (Heb 7:25). We need the Son to have the same substance as the Father that when we are united to him who is the true, eternally begotten Son, his script becomes our script and we might rightly call out, "Abba, Father!" (Gal 4:6)

Because the Son is eternally generated from the Father and is very God of very God, he was uniquely qualified to separate us from our sin as far as the east is from the west, and he is ever ready to intercede for those who have been united to him. Within the doctrine of eternal generation, the church receives an embarrassment of riches, for in the doctrine of eternal generation and the economic activity that manifests the eternal generation, we participate in none other than our Savior—Jesus Christ the righteous.

---

[20] Van Dixhoorn, *Creeds*, 27.

CHAPTER FIVE

The Lord and Life-Giver
The Procession of the Holy Spirit

We will cheat and give you the punchline—the devotional payoff—at the start of this chapter, because it is just too spectacular to wait until the end. Here is the takeaway: the glorious, beautiful, and most Holy Trinity we have been contemplating in this book *is ours* all because of the Holy Spirit.

The Trinity is the overflowing source of all goodness and joy in our lives because the Trinity is the eternal, infinite, limitless source of wisdom, power, beauty, love, and never-ending life. The Trinity is a fire of white-hot holiness, which burns eternally and never changes or diminishes because it is infinitely strong. In short, the Trinity is the overflowing plentitude of glory, love, holiness, and goodness that ensures our happiness both now and forevermore.

However, in our sinful condition, we fallen creatures remain outside of that divine life and love. Without the person and work of the Holy Spirit, we are prevented from enjoying this infinitely joyful God, cut off from the divine beauty of the Trinity on account of our sin. Even the work of Christ, apart from the Spirit, remains *outside of us*. Christ has atoned for our sins, granted us his perfect righteousness, and restored our fellowship with God once again, but apart from the Spirit, all of that redemption accomplished remains external to us. We remain strangers of God without the Spirit. The Holy Spirit is the One who unites us to Christ. The work of our Savior is applied to us by the perfecting power of the Spirit so that by the grace of God we can participate in this triune life.

Throughout the Scriptures, God offers this promise: "I will be their God, and they will be my people" (see, for example, Jer 31:33). And he makes good on this promise in the person and work of the Holy Spirit. God the Spirit says, "I will be *your God*," and we, in and by the Spirit of Christ, respond, "Yes, and *we will be your people*." As one theologian has said, "The Spirit's abiding interest is to bind us to Christ and to his Father, our Father, thereby leading everyone back to the Father through the Son."[1]

Fighting the Spirit

Throughout this book, we have made frequent references to the early centuries of the church and the controversies that shook her members. Arius and his followers have received the majority of our attention, but at this point it is worth mentioning that the followers of Arius were not the only troublemakers during that period. Another controversial figure, and one that necessitated the Council of Constantinople in 381, was Constantinople's own bishop, Macedonius. This bishop had a heretical sect named after him as well, though it is far less memorable than Arius's *Arianism*.

---

[1] Christopher R. J. Holmes, *The Holy Spirit*, New Studies in Dogmatics (Grand Rapids: Zondervan, 2015), 19.

Macedonius's followers were dubbed the apt designation of the *Pneumatomachi* or the "Spirit-fighters." If the Arians denied the eternal generation of the Son, these early Christian heretics denied the eternal spiration of the Holy Spirit and therefore refused to *worship* the Holy Spirit.

The three most popular detractors of the Pneumatomachi were Gregory of Nyssa, his older brother Basil of Caesarea, and their companion Gregory of Nazianzus, who have been grouped together under the designation "The Cappadocian Fathers." The most direct and concentrated work against the Pneumatomachi was Basil's little work, *On the Holy Spirit*. Basil explains, "Lately when I pray with the people, some of those present observed that I render the glory due to God in both ways, namely, to the Father, with the Son together with the Holy Spirit, and to the Father, through the Son, in the Holy Spirit. They said that we used foreign and contradictory words."[2]

According to Basil, his opponents read much into specific prepositions in the biblical text to justify ranking the Spirit as below the Father and Son and therefore undeserving of worship. "Their contention," explains Basil, "is that any mention of Father, Son, and Holy Spirit as dissimilar makes it easy to demonstrate that they are different in nature."[3] For example, Paul says in 1 Cor 8:6 that all things are "*from*" the Father "*through*" the Son, which implies, in their thinking, that the Father and Son are distinct in nature. Basil writes, "They assign 'from whom' to God the—Father—as if it were some lot assigned to—him—but they define God the Son with 'through whom' and the Holy Spirit with 'in whom.'

---

[2] Basil, *On the Holy Spirit*, trans. Stephen Hildebrand (Yonkers, NY: St Vladimir's Seminary Press, 2011), 1.3.

[3] Basil, 2.4.

Moreover, Aëtius says that this use of words never changes, so that, as I have said, the difference in nature is revealed by the difference in expression."[4]

Basil then takes his reader through a master class on linguistics and hermeneutics, showing with *exhaustive* detail that his opponents are simply playing word games. *This simply is not how language works.* Prepositions themselves don't mean anything; they are unintelligible apart from their semantic context. In addition to demonstrating how the biblical record uses each of the prepositions in question ("from," "through," "in," and "by") with respect to each divine person, Basil also calls close attention to the *logic* of the Scriptures.[5] In other words, the Spirit is not only divine according to the Bible's explicit attribution (although there is ample scriptural reason for concluding this much), he is also *treated* as divine in the way the Scriptures talk *about* him. For example, Basil writes:

> All things thirsting for holiness turn to Him [John 4:24]; everything living in virtue never turns away from Him. He waters them with His life-giving breath and helps them reach their proper fulfillment. He perfects all other things, and Himself lacks nothing; He gives life to all things, and is never depleted. He does not increase by additions, but is always complete, self-established and present everywhere. He is the source of sanctification, spiritual light, who gives illumination to everyone using His powers to search the truth—and the illumination He gives is Himself.[6]

---

[4] Basil, 2.4.
[5] For his discussion on the prepositions, see Basil, 3.1–8.21.
[6] Basil, 9.22.

Basil's friend Gregory of Nazianzus was no stranger to the fight over the Spirit either. In his "Oration 31," or, "the Fifth Theological Oration: On the Holy Spirit," he addresses his polemical remarks to his interlocutor, who asks, "What do you say . . . about the Holy Spirit? Where did you get this strange, unscriptural 'God' you are bringing in?"[7] Gregory offers his defense of the Spirit's consubstantiality with the Father and the Son in much the same way as Basil,[8] defending the worship of the Spirit like so:

> It is the Spirit in whom we worship and through whom we pray. "God," it says, "is Spirit, and they who worship him must worship him in Spirit and in Truth" [John 4:24]. And again: "We do not know how to pray as we ought, but the Spirit himself intercedes for us with sighs too deep for words" [Rom 8:26]. And again: "I will pray with the Spirit but I will pray with the mind also" [1 Cor 14:15]—meaning, in mind and spirit. Worshipping, then, and praying in the Spirit seem to me to be simply the Spirit presenting prayer and worship to himself.[9]

Gregory knew that this kind of reasoning would not satisfy his theological rivals, whose biblicist craving for crude propositional summaries was positively insatiable. "Time and time again," Gregory complains, "you repeat the argument about *not being in the Bible*."[10] Rather than catering to the Pneumatomachi's demand

---

[7] Gregory of Nazianzus, "The Fifth Theological Oration (Oration 31): On the Holy Spirit," trans. Lionel Wickham in *On God and Christ: The Five Theological Orations and Two Letters to Cledonius* (Crestwood, NY: St Vladimir's Seminary Press, 2002), 31.1.

[8] See, in particular, Gregory of Nazianzus, 31.20.

[9] Gregory of Nazianzus, 31.12.

[10] Gregory of Nazianzus, 31.21.

for what they might consider "clear passages," Gregory turns the tables on them and demonstrates how this simply is not the way the Scriptures talk about God. Gregory is so profound he deserves to be quoted at length:

> Some things mentioned in the Bible are not factual; some factual things are not mentioned; some nonfactual things receive no mention there; some things are both factual and mentioned. Do you ask for my proofs here? I am ready to offer them. In the Bible, God "sleeps" [Ps 44(43):23(24)], "wakes up" [Jer 31(38):26], "is angered" [Ps 79(78):5, cf. Isa 5:25], "walks" [Gen 3:8], and has a "throne of cherubim" [Isa 37:16; Ps 80(79):1(2)]. Yet when has God ever been subject to emotion? When do you ever hear that God is a bodily being? This is a nonfactual, mental picture. We have used names derived from human experience and applied them, so far as we could, to aspects of God. His retirement from us, for reasons known to himself into an almost unconcerned inactivity, is his "sleeping." Human sleeping, after all, has the character of restful inaction. . . . God's swift motion we call "flight" [Ps 18(17):10(11)]; his watching over us is his "face" [Ps 4:6(7); 34(33):16(17)]; his giving and receiving is his "hand" [Ps 145(144):16]. Indeed every faculty or activity of God has given us a corresponding picture in terms of something bodily.[11]

In other words, in response to his opponents' objection to the Bible's apparent lack of clarity on the Spirit's divine personhood, Gregory essentially says, "Take it up with the Scriptures. You're demanding

---

[11] Gregory of Nazianzus, 31:22.

that the Scriptures talk about the Spirit's being God in a way that Scripture doesn't talk about God *at all*."

The Scriptures reveal infinite truths to us in finite ways with finite language. This *must* be the case. Were God to reveal infinite truths in infinite ways with infinite language, he would not be addressing *us* at all, but only himself. Why? Because *God alone is infinite*. The finite cannot circumscribe or comprehend the infinite. This means, if God is going to reveal himself to us *at all* (let alone the mysterious inner depths of trinitarian relations), he has to do so by way of analogy. So, taking our cue from the Cappadocians, we look to the Scriptures, the self-revelation of the infinite and incomprehensible God, refusing to demand that he conform to our standards of "clarity" regarding the Spirit. Rather, we follow the Scripture's inherent logic and allow the finitude of human words to lead us analogously back up to their ultimate and infinite source.

We begin with John 16—an important passage—where Christ introduces his disciples to the person and work of the Spirit. As in previous chapters, we will briefly examine this passage on its face, and then we will dig deeper to consider its implications for what we can know about the life of God, before coming back to apply the doctrine of the Trinity to our hearts.

Words of Comfort and Hope in a Dark Hour

John 16 is an invitation to the final moments Jesus shared with his disciples before his death on the cross. By that time, he had officially concluded his public ministry, and everything we read about in chapters 12–17 of John's Gospel occurred in the presence of Jesus's disciples alone. These are deeply intimate chapters. Jesus knew what was about to happen, but they did not. They did not know that the very next day, they would see their Teacher, their friend, their Messiah, nailed to a cross, gurgling and coughing up his own blood. They did not know that in a matter of hours, they would watch him say, "It is finished," before bowing his head and giving up his spirit (John 19:30). But Jesus knew. So, Jesus, his heart brimming with love and compassion for his clueless friends, left them with intimate words of comfort, instruction, and hope.

Painful as it may be, the ascension was necessary for the disciples to receive the Holy Spirit. He had to leave first and then send the Holy Spirit to them before they could receive him. Why? It is not as if the Spirit is *unable* to indwell believers who see Jesus in the flesh, as if only one person of the Trinity can be with the people of God at a time. God is omnipresent, and the triune God works inseparably as one. So why must Jesus leave in order for the disciples to receive the Spirit? The reason has everything to do with the work of the gospel that Jesus was sent to accomplish in the flesh. Think of it this way: the Holy Spirit is a benefit of the new covenant that we receive as a result of Christ's high priestly work, which was not complete until he ascended into the heavens to appear before the Father as our intercessor, mediating by means of his own blood! In other words, Jesus had to offer up his blood as the payment for this gift: the Holy Spirit. So, when Jesus told his disciples, "It is better for you if I leave" (John 16:7, paraphrased), he was saying, "If I don't leave you and ascend into heaven, the Holy Spirit will not descend to indwell you. I must leave you so that I can complete my duties as your High Priest and you can receive this gift of the Holy Spirit."

Now the questions to ask are: What makes the Holy Spirit such an amazing gift? Why is the Holy Spirit inside us a better gift than Jesus beside us? Since God is infinite in all his perfections, the benefits of receiving the Holy Spirit to indwell us are literally *limitless*, but one of the benefits that is relevant to this text occurred earlier in John's Gospel when Jesus said, "If you love me, you will keep my commands. And I will ask the Father, and he will give you another Counselor to be with you forever. He is the Spirit of truth. The world is unable to receive him because it doesn't see him or know him. But you do know him, because he remains with you and will be in you" (14:15–17). Then Jesus said, "If anyone loves me, he will keep my word. My Father will love him, and we will come to him and make our home with him" (14:23). If Jesus is right, then we do not have to choose between having Jesus or having the Holy Spirit. If we have the Holy Spirit, we have the Son and the Father as well. In fact, the connection is so intimate that we can say the Holy Trinity is *with us*. The Holy Spirit is the One who supernaturally unites us to Christ—the Vine—and facilitates communion with the triune God.

In chapter 16, Jesus goes on to describe the Spirit's mission when he descends at Pentecost. His ministry on the earth is to convict the world of sin (vv. 8–11), guide the disciples of Jesus into all truth (vv. 12–13), and, preeminently, glorify Jesus. How will the Spirit glorify Jesus? "[The Spirit] will glorify me," says Christ, "for he will take what is mine and declare it to you. All that the Father has is mine; therefore I said that he will take what is mine and declare it to you" (vv. 14–15 ESV). Consider what Christ is saying: the Spirit is going to glorify Jesus. He showcases and presents the glory of Jesus. He calls attention to and adorns the glory of Jesus. And the Spirit does this not separately or indifferently or outside of *his own presence.* Consider this insight from the church father, Basil the Great: "When through his illuminating power we fix our eyes on the beauty of the image of the unseen God, and through the image are led up to the more than beautiful vision of the archetype, his Spirit of knowledge is somehow inseparably present. He supplies to those who love to see the truth the power to see the image in himself. He does not make the manifestation from the outside, but in himself leads to knowledge."[12]

The glory that belongs to Christ—the glory that is *"all the Father has"*—the Spirit then communicates to us by means of his own presence. Now think about what this means for the Spirit. The content of the Spirit's glorifying ministry of the Son is "all that the Father has." All that the Father has is the Son's, and all that the Father and Son have is then declared to us by none other than the Holy Spirit. Yet unless the Spirit also possesses all that is common to the Father and the Son, he cannot accomplish this great work within us. From behind the veil of our creatureliness, the Spirit brings forth the glory of the divine—the Father and the Son—which he could not do unless that glory is his as well.

How appropriate then for Paul to write to the Corinthians and describe the Spirit in this way: "Now God has revealed these things to us by the Spirit, since the Spirit searches everything, even the depths of God. For who knows a person's thoughts except his spirit within him? In the same way, no one knows the thoughts of God except the Spirit of God. Now we have not received the spirit of the world, but the Spirit who comes from God, so that we may understand what has been freely given to us by God" (1 Cor 2:10–12). The Spirit reveals what is *his*—this is why the Nicene Creed confesses that the Spirit is the Lord and Life-Giver, "who with the Father and the Son together is worshiped and glorified."[13]

What does all of this mean for our contemplation of the Trinity? When we look at the Creator's work in history, the infinite is revealed to the finite but in ways that accommodate us as creatures. God is no *less* than what he reveals in human history (he truly reveals *himself*),

---

[12] Basil, *On the Holy Spirit*, 18.47.

[13] Chad Van Dixhoorn, *Creeds, Confessions, and Catechisms: A Reader's Edition* (Wheaton, IL: Crossway, 2022), 18.

but he is certainly more—he is, after all, incomprehensible. A small dose of philosophy can help. The language about God in Scripture is not univocal. *Univocal* language occurs when there is essentially a one-to-one correlation. For example, if someone says, "I went to the restroom at home, so I do not need to use the restroom here," the word "restroom" in both uses signifies the same thing. *Equivocal* language occurs when the same word can be used to signify totally different things. For example, "I went into the attic with a bat to fight the bat flying around up there." Here, we may use the same word ("bat") but it means something else with each use. *Analogical* language is language that has both similarity and dissimilarity. When we say, "Our pastor is a *good* man, and we just ate some *good* steak," there is something about both uses of the word "good" that corresponds, even if the uses differ in other ways. What does this detour have to do with the Trinity? All our language about God, in the Scriptures and in theology, works by way of *analogy*. Here's the point: when we talk about God, the referent is never *less* than what we describe but always infinitely *more*. Humans may have wisdom, and God is wise, but his wisdom is infinitely beyond our wisdom—it is not simply different in degree but in kind. Furthermore, whereas we have wisdom by participation in God, God has wisdom by nature—he *is* all-wise (see chapter 3 on simplicity).

For this reason, we must be careful lest we assume that a description of the Trinity in the history of redemption projects something back up into God in an exhaustive, timeless sense. For example, during the incarnation, the Son humbled himself and submitted to the mission given to him by the Father for the sake of accomplishing our redemption. Does that mean that the eternal Trinity in and of itself, apart from the economy of salvation, is divided between an authoritative person and a subordinate person? Not at all. Such a view creates a hierarchy in the Trinity and fails to recognize that "authority" is a divine attribute that the Father, Son, and Spirit share in common—they are one in essence, will, power, and glory. Nevertheless, by virtue of his humanity, the Son's earthly, human humiliation is fitting. For the same Son who was sent into our world by the Father is begotten by the Father from eternity (see chapter 4). There is, in other words, a fitting correspondence.

A similar principle can be applied to the Spirit. For example, the Spirit is named *Spirit*—in the Greek, it's the same word for "breath" or "wind." According to Jesus in John 3, there is something about the analogy of a person breathing out air, or wind blowing through trees, that fittingly corresponds to the Spirit's *proceeding* (or being *spirated*) from the Father and Son from all eternity. As we learned in chapters 1 and 2, it is for this reason that we say the Spirit's eternal relation of origin is spiration. Yet Scripture does not only describe the Spirit with imagery like "breath" or "wind." If it did, we might assume that the Spirit is an impersonal force like electricity. Scripture also describes the Spirit in a number of other ways. Consider two of the primary names Scripture attributed to the Spirit: *Love* and *Gift*.

The Spirit Is Love

Love is a divine attribute, which means it is an attribute of the one divine essence the three persons have in common—or rather, the divine nature of the three persons *is,* simply, *love*. It is not as if the Spirit has more love than the Father and the Son—they are one in essence, will, power, and glory, which means they are one in divine love. However, certain attributes like love may be appropriated by certain persons of the Trinity. Love is a divine attribute that we properly ascribe to Father, Son, and Spirit; nonetheless, the Spirit is described *as* divine love. That is fitting since this is the Spirit who proceeds as love from the Father (Lover) and the Son (the Beloved).

That mysterious truth has profound implications for us. In Romans 5, Paul says that we have peace with God through Christ, and therefore we can rejoice in our sufferings, "knowing that suffering produces endurance, and endurance produces character, and character produces hope, and hope does not put us to shame, *because God's love has been poured into our hearts through the Holy Spirit who has been given to us*" (vv. 3–5 ESV; emphasis added). The love of God is ours because *the Spirit of God has been given to us*. To receive the Spirit of God is to have divine love *poured into our hearts*.

Here is the important point: the Spirit is the Father's love for the Son and the Son's love for the Father. The application is marvelous: when we receive the Spirit, we receive the Father and Son *in love*. We are *brought into* divine, trinitarian love.

The Spirit Is Gift

Not only is the Spirit described as *love*, but in John's Gospel the Spirit is described as *gift*. In John 3:34, Jesus is designated as the One whom God sent to speak God's words and *give the Spirit* without measure. In John 4 and 7, the Spirit is described as an overflowing river of life. Additionally, in the book of Acts, we read about believers receiving the "gift of the Holy Spirit" (2:38; 10:45). If the Spirit *is* the divine gift, is it any wonder, then, why the gifts the church receives are associated with the Spirit? In 1 Corinthians 12–14, the Spirit's generous presence is manifested by administering gifts that build up the church: the members edify one another with the gifts that the Spirit graciously gives. In Galatians 5 the Spirit produces fruit in the lives of those who walk in his generous leading. The

Spirit, in the life of the local church, is the manifestation of the Trinity's infinite, self-giving generosity.

In all of these examples, the Spirit's eternal relation of origin—spiration from the Father and Son—is a "double procession." The Spirit is "breathed out" eternally by *both* Father and Son. Remember that what distinguishes the Father, Son, and Spirit in the Trinity is their eternal relations of origin (see chapters 1 and 2). The Father, who is unbegotten, eternally begets the Son, and the Spirit eternally proceeds from the Father *and* Son. This is a pattern hinted at across Scripture. Sometimes the Spirit is described as the Spirit *of the Father* (cf., Matt 10:20), and sometimes the Spirit is described as the Spirit *of the Son* (cf., Gal 4:6) (more on this "double procession" as the chapter continues). The medieval poet Dante captured the Spirit's relation to the Father and the Son in his *Paradiso*, the final part of his masterpiece, *The Divine Comedy*.

> Within the depthless deep and clear existence
> of that abyss of light three circles shone—
> three in color, one in circumference:
>
> the second from the first, rainbow from rainbow;
> the third, an exhalation of pure fire
> equally breathed forth by the other two.[14]

The God of the creeds is the God Dante beautifully describes here. He is, paradoxically, a "depthless deep" and "clear existence." His incomprehensible nature is an "abyss," but it is not an abyss of *nothingness*—empty and void of life. His is an "abyss of *light*." Within the inner life of this God—the "one God in Trinity and

---

[14] Dante Alighieri, *The Divine Comedy: The Inferno, The Purgatorio, The Paradiso*, trans. John Ciardi (New York: New American Library, 2003), *Paradiso*, Canto XXXIII.115–20.

Trinity in unity," the "three in color, one in circumference"—the Son is *from* the Father ("the second *from* the first") and is *Light from Light*. Is it not fitting to describe this eternal generation as "rainbow from rainbow"? And who is the Spirit? He is "an exhalation of *pure fire / equally breathed forth by the other two*."

If the Spirit proceeds from the Father and the Son, then this same Spirit can speak through the prophets of old to reveal the Father and the Son for the sake of our salvation. The last paragraph of the Nicene Creed not only says the Spirit is the Lord and Life-Giver, one who should be worshipped together with the Father and the Son, but the creed also says *the Spirit* "spoke by the prophets." *The Spirit* is God's saving goodness communicated to *us* sinners. *The Spirit* is the One who baptizes us into Christ for the remission of sins. *The Spirit* leads us into truth through the teaching of the apostles he inspired. And *the Spirit* turns us into one, holy, catholic, and apostolic church, as the creed says.

Let us make things personal: think about your own conversion to Christ. When you became a believer, you trusted in the cross of Christ, persuaded you desperately needed his atonement for the forgiveness of your sins. And when you heard the gospel—the good news about the life, death, and resurrection of Christ—you received it with joy. But most of us did not accept that good news the first time we heard it. Why? Did Jesus somehow change from when you ignored the gospel to the first time you said, "I need Jesus"? No, the change was entirely owing to the generous, self-giving, irresistibly sweet ministry of the Holy Spirit. At some point, the Spirit breathed new spiritual life within—in theology we call this "regeneration"—summoning you to participate in the everlasting life of the Trinity. As the One who proceeds eternally from the Father and the Son, the Spirit leads us into the love the Father has shown to us in the grace of his Son.

The Spirit is the Consummator and the Perfecter, the absolute expression of God's infinite generosity. He adorned and glorified creation when he hovered over the face of the waters—the Father created the cosmos through the Son by the Spirit. The Spirit not only anointed kings and priests but spoke through the prophets, promising a Savior to God's people. And when the angel announced to the virgin the advent of God's only begotten Son, Mary was found to be with child *from the Holy Spirit*. The Spirit anointed the man Christ Jesus, the Second Adam, as he fulfilled his redemptive ministry on earth, until the time came for him to walk the road of Calvary by the power of the Spirit. Vindicated on the third day, Christ bodily rose from the grave by the power of the Spirit.

When Jesus ascended into heaven, the Spirit descended at Pentecost just as Jesus promised. He applied Christ's redemption to God's people, granting us by grace the divine life he shares eternally with the Father and the Son by nature. The Spirit who has united us to Christ has baptized us into the body of Christ—the one, holy, catholic, and apostolic church. As the divine gift from the Father and the Son, the Spirit fills the church with gifts so that all those whom he has united to Christ are conformed into the image of God's Son. The Spirit teaches us the Scriptures, revealing to us the depths of God so that by the Spirit's illumination our minds behold the beauty of Christ, until we one day see the glory of Christ in the beatific vision. The Spirit facilitates communion with Christ and all those in union and communion with him—the church. This communion occurs when we participate in his body and blood by the breaking of bread and the drinking of wine at the Lord's Table—for there, the Spirit seats us with Christ in heaven to dine with him. When the saint comes to Christ *through the Spirit* and by faith, he or she feeds on Christ in a sense, but God feeds Christ to the believer in quite another, more tangible sense after he has been baptized into Christ's earthly body. For there, in that local expression of the universal body of Christ, the believer's faithful feasting on Christ is punctuated in a physical dimension; he is spiritually nourished with real bread and real wine as he continues to feed on Christ by faith, and it is the Spirit who makes it so. And one day, the Spirit, who raised Christ from the dead, will also give life to our mortal bodies and bring to completion a new heaven and earth.

The *Filioque*

Taking the totality of biblical metaphors (e.g., the Spirit as divine *love*, divine *breath*, divine *wind*, divine *gift*, divine *bright cloud*, the One who *overshadows*, the One who hovers over the waters, etc.), we conclude that: (1) the Spirit is divine, bearing a timelessly eternal relation to the Father and the Son, and (2) his relation to the Father is distinct from the Son's relation to the Father. So, the Spirit is not *generated* by the Father but is rather *breathed* out by the Father and the Son.

Of course, saying "and the Son" calls our attention to a hotly contested debate between the theological traditions of the East and those of the West. The phrase "and the Son" (or, "*filioque*") is an addition to the Nicene-Constantinopolitan Creed that was included at the Council of Toledo in AD 589. By this point in the history of Christendom, the Roman Empire had already divided into the Western kingdom (which was eventually taken over by the Ostrogoths when Rome was sacked by the "barbarians") and the Eastern Byzantine kingdom, known as Byzantium. Churches in the Western kingdom predominantly spoke Latin, and churches in the Eastern kingdom mostly spoke Greek. The Council of Toledo was a Latin-speaking council in the Western kingdom, and so the Eastern churches were marginalized by default and were not included. The Council of Toledo was thus *not* a truly *ecumenical* council, though it purported to be just that.

Still, while this council provoked the churches of Byzantium, a general and external unity was maintained for several more centuries. By the eleventh century, the bishop of Rome had accumulated much power in the West, and the doctrine of the papacy had emerged. For generations, the popes of Rome insisted that the *filioque* was definitional for orthodoxy, and eventually, Pope Leo IX and Michael Cerularius (the patriarch of Constantinople) excommunicated each other over the issue in 1054. This is what historians describe as the "Great Schism."

Interestingly enough, up until that time, the Eastern churches were content to recognize Rome—and the bishop of Rome—in a sort of privileged position: they recognized a *kind of* Roman primacy. But they *never* recognized the papacy as infallible.[15] In other words, the Eastern Church did not recognize Rome's claim to *universal dominion*, which is to say that the schism is not only a result of the theological dispute over the *filioque*. The disputes were also ecclesiological and political in nature. Regardless of the circumstantial reasons for the schism, however, the *filioque* continues to be a dividing issue between Roman Catholicism and Eastern Orthodoxy.

In assessing the situation, our sympathies lie with the Eastern Church's objection to papal overreach, and the Western Church's

---

[15] John Anthony McGuckin, for example, notes, "The East saw Rome's primacy of honor as following from its (former) role as center of the imperial administration. Rome, on the other hand, saw its popes having a primacy of jurisdiction following from its particular charism as the see of saint Peter and home of the earliest Christian martyrs." John Anthony McGuckin, *The Path of Christianity: The First Thousand Years* (Grand Rapids: IVP Academic, 2017), 525.

theological distinctives. Without the *filioque*, there is a danger of affirming a kind of separation of the Son from the Spirit. During and after the *filioque* controversy, many in the East came to articulate what we regard as a less preferable portrayal of eternal processions. For such theologians, the Son relates eternally to the Father as the One who is eternally generated from the Father, and the Spirit relates eternally to the Father in the sense that he is eternally spirated from the Father, but the Son and Spirit do not really relate eternally to *one another*. In contrast to this perspective, the *filioque* preserves the Spirit's eternal relation not only to the Father but also to the Son, without conflating the Father's and Son's respective personal properties of paternity and filiation.

Additionally, the *filioque* has a clear biblical and analogical logic. We can arrive at the idea of the *filioque* by reasoning analogically from the divine economy in much the same way that we arrive at the idea of the Son's eternal generation from his economic actions. The Son is sent by the Father because he is the One who is eternally generated by the Father. The Father *and* Son give the Holy Spirit because the Holy Spirit is *eternally spirated* by the Father and the Son. It is difficult to pick one of these conclusions without the other. The *filioque* has a trinitarian logic that makes good sense of eternal generation *and* spiration within the context of eternal generation. In eternal generation, the Father gives the Son to have life in himself—he receives from the Father all that the Father is, *including* the Father's spiration of the Spirit. In this way, the Spirit proceeds from the Father and the Son, but not in the same manner. He proceeds from the Father and from the Son *through* the Son's generation from the Father. The Son's spiration of the Spirit is something he receives from the Father eternally in generation.

Not only does the *filioque* help us with our theology proper, it also makes sense of our understanding of salvation and union with Christ.

Union with Christ is our access point to life in the triune God, and there is no union with Christ without the Spirit. Again, the punchline of this chapter, given at the beginning, is that because of the Spirit, the Trinity is made *ours*. The Spirit is our bond to Christ. And here is the idea: this bond of salvation has an analogue in the Godhead—it is the Spirit that proceeds eternally from the Son so that it is the Spirit who unites us *to* the Son. The Spirit's mission in the economy of salvation comes from the Father and Son. Therefore, the Spirit unites us to the Father through the Son, which *fittingly reflects* the intra-trinitarian taxis (or, *order*) of the divine life flowing from the Father through the Son, and from the Father and Son to the Spirit. Consider these glorious words from the eighteenth-century hymnist, John Kent, who puts this union in its trinitarian and pneumatological context:

> This sacred bond shall never break,
> Though earth should to her center shake;
> Rest, doubting saint, assured of this,
> For God has pledged His holiness.
>
> He swore but once the deed was done;
> 'Twas settled by the Three in One;
> Christ was appointed to redeem
> All that the Father loved in Him.
>
> Hail, sacred union, firm and strong
> How great thy grace, how sweet the song,
> That rebel worms should ever be
> One with incarnate Deity!
>
> One in the tomb, one when He rose,
> One when he triumphed o'er His foes
> One when in heav'n He took His seat,
> While seraphs sung at hell's defeat.

> Blessed by the wisdom and the grace,
> Th' eternal love and faithfulness,
> That's in the gospel scheme revealed,
> And is by God the Spirit sealed.[16]

The wisdom, grace, love, and faithfulness revealed in the gospel scheme is *sealed* by none other than the Spirit. Through him, we have Christ as our Brother and God as our Father. In his recent book on the Trinity in the book of Revelation, Brandon D. Smith puts his finger on this trinitarian-soteriological point when he writes, "Our vision of the triune God fittingly finds its culmination in the Holy Spirit. He is the marvelous gatekeeper to God's throne room, the one who opens John's eyes to the wonders of heaven, and speaks alongside the Son as the promised comforter."[17]

The Spirit and Groaning

We cannot emphasize enough how important the Spirit's eternal relation to the Father and Son is for informing and empowering the Christian life. Even at the level of prayer, the Spirit himself empowers and translates our prayers in this pilgrimage through the Christian life. Consider this passage from Romans 8: "In the same way the Spirit also helps us in our weakness, because we do not know what to pray for as we should, but the Spirit himself intercedes for us with inexpressible groanings. And he who searches our hearts knows the mind of the Spirit, because he intercedes for

---

[16] John Kent (1766–1843), "'Twixt Jesus and the Chosen Race," hymn, public domain.

[17] Brandon D. Smith, *The Trinity in the Book of Revelation: Seeing Father, Son, and Holy Spirit in John's Apocalypse* (Downers Grove, IL: IVP Academic, 2022), 138.

the saints according to the will of God" (vv. 26–27). This passage begins with the phrase "in the same way," harkening us back, of course, to the previous passage, which was all about the hope of glory. The preceding verses in Romans 8 speak of the groaning of those who groan inwardly, and the groaning of creation itself. What are the groanings *for*? What do we and creation groan *after*? "The redemption of our bodies" (v. 23). The whole momentum of the preceding verses of Romans, in other words, points us forward to the future glory that is promised to us who have the Spirit of him who raised Christ Jesus from the dead. Paul concludes that section with, "Now in this hope we were saved, but hope that is seen is not hope, because who hopes for what he sees? Now if we hope for what we do not see, we eagerly wait for it with patience" (vv. 24–25). And now Paul says, "In the same way," which means, whatever he is about to say, it will involve *hope in the future* and *patience in the present*.

Within this context, Paul speaks of the Spirit helping us in our weakness. What weakness? The weakness of *perplexity in our prayer life*. We do not know what to pray for as we ought, "but the Spirit himself intercedes for us with inexpressible groanings" (v. 26). So, this is how the Spirit helps us when we do not know what to pray for: *he prays for us*. And he does so—he intercedes for us—*with "inexpressible groanings."* That is what he intercedes *with*. He takes *"groanings,"* and he brings them to God for us. Now, what are these "groanings"? Whose are they? We know the Spirit is bringing them to God in an act of intercession when we, in our weakness, do not know what to pray for as we ought, *but what are they?* Are they *our* groanings, or are they the *Spirit's* groanings?

There are good reasons for us to say "yes" to that "either/or" question. That is, there is a sense in which these groanings are ours *and* the Spirit's, though not in the same way. On the one hand, this chapter has already said a great deal about our groaning, so it is natural for us to read this "groaning" as a continuation of what has come before. And on the other hand, we have to remember that what the Spirit is doing here is *acting on our behalf to account for our inadequacies*. The point is that *we do not know what to pray for*, and the Spirit is praying for us in our stead. Coming together, it looks something like this: While we wait on this side of glory, we wait eagerly as those who are weak and perplexed—so weak and perplexed that we often do not even know what to pray for. But God is so *for us* that he has given us his own Spirit, who stirs up and translates those "beyond-description groanings" into prayers on our behalf. We can get a hint of this from the following verse: "And he who searches our hearts knows the mind of the Spirit, because he intercedes for the saints according to the will of God" (Rom 8:27). So these intercessions are apparently something God finds when he "searches our hearts." God searches hearts, and *there*, in our hearts, he finds these intercessions, and in finding those intercessions, he finds "the mind of the Spirit."

To help grasp the weight of this, let's try to paint a picture that we trust is familiar to many. There you are: absolutely perplexed by some trial or sin or season of suffering, lamenting the weakness of your flesh. You are paralyzed. You do not even know what to pray for, but you know you should. So, you sit down, close your eyes, and you try to form a word or a thought, but you come up short, and you shake your head. You are at a loss. Meanwhile—*while that pathetic scene is taking place*—God is searching your heart, and what he finds there is the Holy Spirit *praying for you*, giving to the Father the wordless groans that you cannot articulate. An intra-trinitarian conversation of perfect understanding is taking place *on your behalf*, while you are fretting about not knowing what to pray for. And he does all of this *"according to the will of God"* (v. 27).

Recall, for example, how we learned to pray from Jesus in the garden of Gethsemane: "If it be your will . . ." (Luke 22:42, paraphrased). He prayed that way as a human so that we might have a sinless human who could be our perfect sacrifice. But he also prayed that way to teach us how to be faithful humans. And faithful humans are invited to pray for, and about, anything and everything, with the qualifier "If it be your will." We cannot be certain everything we ask for is God's will. Although we want the thing we are asking for, nevertheless we want his will even more. So even those prayers are helpful because they bring *us* and *our will* into alignment with God and his will. God is shaping us always, with every prayer. But here is the breathtaking point we learn from Rom 8:26–27: the Spirit never has to issue that qualifier. When he prays for us, all of his prayers are *"according to the will of God."* And this means all of them are intercessions that *will* be answered in the affirmative.

And remember, these promises are for those *in Christ Jesus,* for whom "there is therefore now no condemnation" (Rom 8:1 ESV). When God did for us what the law, weakened by the flesh, could not do (i.e., when he sent Christ in the likeness of sinful flesh and for sin condemned *our* sin in *his* flesh on the cross), he was making it possible for his Spirit to indwell us. And now, since "the Spirit of him who raised Jesus from the dead dwells in [us], he who raised Christ Jesus from the dead *will also* give life to [our] mortal bodies through his Spirit who dwells in [us]" (v. 11 ESV; emphasis added). One of the ways he comes through for us on this promise is by *interceding for us with groanings too deep for words, according to the will of God.* Christ is the vehicle, the Father and his will is the destination, and the Spirit is the driver. *In* Christ, the Spirit *gets us there.*

How can we take the Holy Spirit for granted when he has given us everything?

Worship in Spirit and Truth

In John 4, Jesus spoke with a Samaritan woman at the well, instructing her how to worship God. "But an hour is coming, and is now here, when the true worshipers will worship the Father in Spirit and in truth. Yes, the Father wants such people to worship him" (v. 23).

Many assume Jesus was merely speaking about the internal disposition of the worshipper. The Samaritans and the Jews disputed over the proper location of worship, but Jesus told this Samaritan woman that location is irrelevant. The time has come for worshippers to glorify God "in spirit and in truth"—in sincerity and knowledge. *True enough.* But most Christians in the history of the church insisted that Jesus was saying far more. After all, *Spirit* and *Truth* are both names that Scripture elsewhere—in the very same book, even—attributes to the Second and Third Persons of the Trinity. The church father Basil writes, "If we say that worship offered *in* the Son (the truth) is worship offered *in* the Father's image, we can say the same about worship offered *in* the Spirit since the Spirit in himself reveals the divinity of the Lord. The Holy Spirit cannot be divided from the Father and the Son in worship. If you remain outside the Spirit, you cannot worship at all, and if you are *in* him you cannot separate him from God. Light cannot be separated from what it makes visible, and it is impossible for you to recognize Christ, the image of the invisible God, unless the Spirit enlightens you."[18]

If we love Christ and desire to worship him, then we cannot afford to neglect the Holy Spirit on whom we are utterly dependent. The Spirit, then, is nonnegotiable in our worship of God. When Jude instructs Christians to build themselves up in their most holy

---

[18] Basil, *On the Holy Spirit*, 26.64.

faith, he tells them to pray *in the Holy Spirit*. By doing so, you "keep yourselves in the love of God, waiting expectantly for the mercy of our Lord Jesus Christ for eternal life" (Jude vv. 20–21). Built up in the faith, praying in the Spirit, kept in the love of God—the Christian must hold all three tightly together. But how does one *pray* in the Spirit? And what does it mean to *keep oneself* in the love of God? These are deep mysteries, but whatever they mean, they compel us to stay close to Christ by walking with the Spirit. That journey will take us deeper into the inexhaustible love of God—or as C. S. Lewis once said, further up and further in.[19] Yet that journey begins now as we worship the Trinity by the power of the Spirit.

Such an exciting journey should also galvanize our enthusiasm for the salvation of those who are not followers of Christ, who do not have the Holy Spirit dwelling within. We extend Christ to the world and invite them to come to him with nothing but the empty hands of faith. The promise is grand: God's Spirit will usher you into the love of the Trinity. The apostle Paul says that "no one can say, 'Jesus is Lord,' except by the Holy Spirit" (1 Cor 12:3). As the church, therefore, we summon the world to repentance and faith—faith in the only One who can restore us to fellowship with the Holy Trinity, all while trusting the Holy Spirit to bring the elect into that blessed fellowship. The Spirit and the church say, "Come" (Rev 22:17).

---

[19] See chap. 4, n. 16.

CHAPTER SIX

Communion with the Undivided Trinity
Inseparable Operations

Who created the heavens and the earth?

The most obvious answer to this question is *God* (Gen 1:1). But could we get more specific? What if we ask the question, "Which divine person created the heavens and the earth? The Father, Son, or Holy Spirit?" And to keep the thought experiment going, does our answer change if we multiply our questions with respect to the various actions attributed to God in the Scriptures? Which divine person sustains the heavens of the earth? Which divine person redeems mankind through Christ's atoning sacrifice on the cross? Whose divine wrath is poured out on Christ when he hung suspended by nails to wood at Golgotha? Which divine person answers our prayers? Which divine person will make all things new in the glorification of the cosmos? Which divine person shall we behold in the beatific vision—the blessed hope of seeing God in heaven?

In case it is not clear by now, these are all trick questions. By asking "*which divine* person," we have misled you—we have implied that the answer to these questions can only be one person in distinction from the other two. But—please forgive us for the *temporary* deception!—this is unfair of us. The premise to our questions is incorrect from the start. The answer to all these questions is simply, "God the Trinity." The triune God creates, redeems, and will glorify his creation. The triune God hears and answers prayer. The triune God is the One whom we worship— "The one God in Trinity and the Trinity in unity, neither confounding their persons nor dividing the essence."[1] Which divine person? *Each* and *every*.

Now, while this answer may be satisfactory at the purely theoretical level, the textured presentation of divine *action* in the Scriptures can befuddle us at first glance. How might we maintain both the singularity of divine action on the one hand, and the biblical portrayal of distinguishable divine persons as they carry out divine action on the other?

The ancient Christian principle used by theologians across the great tradition is the doctrine of *inseparable operations*.[2] This doctrine has corollaries as well, including the principle we call *divine appropriations* and the reality of our doxological *communion with the Trinity*. In this chapter, we will define and describe each of

---

[1] "The Athanasian Creed" in Chad Van Dixhoorn, *Creeds, Confessions, and Catechisms: A Reader's Edition* (Wheaton, IL: Crossway, 2022), 21.

[2] For a much fuller treatment on this doctrine, see Adonis Vidu, *The Same God Who Works All Things: Inseparable Operations in Trinitarian Theology* (Grand Rapids: Eerdmans, 2021).

these concepts, and then we will elucidate the glorious doxological point: in Christ, we worship, *and commune with,* "one God in Trinity and the Trinity in unity."

What Is "Inseparable Operations"?

Stated simply, the doctrine of inseparable operations teaches that the external works of the Trinity are undivided (*Opera Trinitatis ad extra sunt indivisa*).[3] Since the Trinity is one, the Trinity's action are one. The actions of God flow from the divine essence, which is common to Father, Son, and Spirit. Augustine states the matter memorably when he writes "the Father, and the Son, and the Holy Spirit, as they are indivisible, so work indivisibly."[4]

Tied up within this doctrine is a classical understanding of the divine will of the Trinity. The idea is that a divine action is the execution of the divine will—if the will of God is one, the action of God must also be one. To deny this principle is to attribute *divine* actions (things that God does) to distinct *wills* or (in modern theological parlance) *centers of consciousness*. But if we affirm three divine willers executing three distinct wills with three distinct sets of action, we fall short of biblical and historical orthodoxy. Taken

---

[3] Richard Muller notes, "Since the Godhead is one in essence, one in knowledge, and one in will, it would be impossible in any work *ad extra* for one of the divine persons to will and to do one thing and another of the divine persons to will or do another." Richard A. Muller, *Dictionary of Latin and Greek Theological Terms: Drawn Principally from Protestant Scholastic Theology*, 2nd ed. (Grand Rapids: Baker Academic, 2017), 246.

[4] Augustine, *De Trinitate,* ed. John E. Rotelle, OSA, and Edmund Hill, OP, 2nd ed. (Hyde Park, NY: New City, 2012), 1.4.7.

to its extreme, we might conclude from this way of thinking that three distinct wills properly belong to *three distinct beings*. Such a conclusion is nothing short of tritheism and must be avoided at all costs.

Yet it *seems* apparent from the biblical text itself that persons of the Trinity work distinctly from one another, does it not? Sometimes you see works attributed to one or two divine persons apart from the other (e.g., where is the Spirit in that great trinitarian passage, 1 Cor 8:4–6?). Sometimes you see persons of the Trinity in *dialogue* with one another (e.g., John 12:28; 17:6–26). In the garden of Gethsemane and on the cross, our Lord Jesus himself, the Second Person of the Trinity, appears even to *object* to the Father's will (e.g., Matt 26:39; 27:46). It would seem from these passages that "the operations" of the Trinity are in fact divisible.

On the other hand, you also see instances of the very same divine action attributed to the distinct persons of the Trinity (e.g., Gen 1:1; cf., John 1:1–3; Col 1:15–18; Heb 1:1–3; Jude v. 5). Jesus will go so far as to attribute an *absolute unity* between his own actions and the actions of the Father (e.g., John 5:17–19). So apparently, in view of *these* passages, the doctrine of inseparable operations is not *merely* the logical deduction of divine simplicity and the conviction of monotheism in the light of New Testament revelation (though it is *at least* that); rather, it announces itself from the very pages of Scripture. We are not merely *compelled* to affirm the doctrine to avoid tritheism, the Scriptures themselves affirm the idea, at least in some way. So when we examine one set of texts, the doctrine seems clearly present, but when we examine another set of texts, the doctrine seems foreign. What are we to do?

The Early Church Origins of Inseparable Operations

As with other doctrines examined in this book, we are not the first Christians to address this topic. It should be no surprise that the doctrine of inseparable operations arose as a conceptual solution of sorts within the trinitarian debates of the fourth century and were subsequently sharpened over the following centuries. Athanasius appealed to this doctrine to defend the Son's divinity against the Arians, in part, by appealing to the Pauline statement in 1 Cor 1:24 that the Son is the "*power* of God" (emphasis added)."[5] This verse does a lot of heavy lifting for Athanasius and other pro-Nicene theologians. Not only does it bear great significance on the Son's timelessly eternal relation to the Father (was there ever a time that the omnipotent God was without *his power*?), but it also implies the singularity of the Father and Son's operation. If the Father's *doing something* is the exercise of his *power*, what then can he do *without* his power? Nothing. Simply put, if the Son is indeed "the power of God," as the apostle Paul says, then there can be no separation whatever between the Father and the Son's divine action.

But that is not all we can say. Like *love*, which functions as *both* a divine attribute and a divine name for the Third Person of the Trinity (as we saw in the previous chapter), *power* is not simply a designation of the Son (as in the case of 1 Cor 1:24). For thinkers like Hilary of Poitiers, Gregory of Nyssa, Gregory of Nazianzus, Augustine, and Ambrose, "Power is a property of the

---

[5] Athanasius, *Against the Arians (NPNF² 4)*, 2.2. For a helpful discussion here, see Khaled Anatolios, *Retrieving Nicaea: The Development and Meaning of Trinitarian Doctrine* (Grand Rapids: Baker Academic, 2018), 116.

divine essence, such that the *homoousios* demands a single divine power."[6] If divine power is a property not unique to one person in distinction from another but rather of the *divine essence*, and if the divine essence *is* the Father (eternally unbegotten), Son (eternally begotten), and Spirit (eternally proceeding from the Father and Son), then the persons of the Trinity *are* divine power. Each person is one, wholly, with the divine essence, and therefore, to attribute divine power to one is to attribute a property shared identically with all three. Divine operations are nothing other than the exercise of divine power. Again, this all positively requires *inseparable operations*.

As we insist on this doctrine, we must be careful not to imply something like modalism. The affirmation of inseparable operations does not collapse all three persons of the Trinity into a single impersonal Subject. To that end, we must be sure to take into consideration the distinct *manner* in which the one, simple divine nature subsists in the three persons of the Trinity. The Father *is* the divine nature. But what is his *mode of subsistence*? He is unbegotten. As the origin in the Godhead, he *eternally begets* his Son though he is begotten by no one. The Son likewise *is that same, simple* divine nature, but according to his mode of subsistence, he is *eternally begotten* from the Father's divine essence. Again, the Spirit is the same, simple divine nature, but according to the Spirit's mode of subsistence, the Spirit eternally proceeds from the Father and Son's divine essence. Remember, there is no divine nature that exists apart from the persons—the divine nature simply *is* Father, Son, and Spirit. The three persons, therefore, are indivisible in their one,

---

[6] D. Glenn Butner Jr., *The Son Who Learned Obedience: A Theological Case against the Eternal Submission of the Son* (Eugene, OR: Pickwick, 2018), 35.

simple divine essence. So too, then, the operations of the Trinity are undivided.

The foregoing is why Basil will affirm in his treatise *On the Holy Spirit*, "In everything the Holy Spirit is indivisible and inseparable from the Father and the Son."[7] He goes on to say, "In their creation, consider for me the initial cause of their existence (the Father), the Maker (the Son), the Perfector (the Spirit). So, the ministering spirits exist by the will of the Father, they are brought into being by the energy of the Son, and they are perfected by the presence of the Spirit."[8] While we may be tempted to read much into Basil's distinct attributions to the persons, we must understand that no *single* divine action ever occurred apart from all three of these "causes." To attribute the "original cause" to the Father, the "creative cause" to the Son, and the "perfecting cause" to the Spirit is not at all to attribute separate, individual, and autonomous operations to each divine person (this would be odd, given that Basil wrote this in *service* of his affirmation of inseparable operations). The distinction between "original," "creative," and "perfecting" causes does not denote *different* actions corresponding to *different* wills. These are rather personal appropriations (an idea we shall return to later in the chapter) of the *same single action* (in this case, the act of creation). Gregory of Nyssa, likewise, put the matter elegantly when he wrote:

> But in the case of the Divine nature we do not similarly learn that the Father does anything by Himself in which the Son does not work conjointly, or again that the Son has any special operation apart from the Holy Spirit; but every operation which extends from God to the Creation, and is

---

[7] Basil, *On the Holy Spirit*, trans. Stephen Hildebrand (Yonkers, NY: St Vladimir's Seminary Press, 2011)

[8] Basil, 16.38.

> named according to our variable conceptions of it, has its origin from the Father, and proceeds through the Son, and is perfected in the Holy Spirit. For this reason the name derived from the operation is not divided with regard to the number of those who fulfil it, because the action of each concerning anything is not separate and peculiar, but whatever comes to pass . . . comes to pass by the action of the Three, yet what does come to pass is not three things.[9]

Those last words are crucial for our purposes here. "Yet what does come to pass is not three things." The triune persons do not merely cooperate with one another, but Father, Son, and Spirit exercise a single will—all operations are *from* the Father, *through* the Son, and *in* the Spirit. Therefore, just as there are not three separate wills in the Trinity, so too we cannot posit separate, autonomous *operations* as such. The will of the Father is the divine will of the Begetter, while the will of the Son is *the same divine* will of the Begotten. In the same way, the actions of the Father are the *divine actions* of the Begetter, while the actions of the Son are *the same divine actions* of the Begotten. Every divine action is an action of the Trinity, which is to say every divine action is the single action of the Unbegotten (Father), Begotten (Son), and Spirated (Spirit). If the Trinity's divine essence is simple, then it should not be a surprise that the operations of the Trinity are inseparable.

Since the Trinity is one, the Trinity acts as one. This, in a nutshell, *is* the doctrine of inseparable operations. Another way of summarizing the doctrine is to put it in the dictum of a hermeneutical

---

[9] Gregory of Nyssa, *On "Not Three Gods,"* in *A Select Library of Nicene and Post-Nicene Fathers of the Christian Church*, ed. Philip Schaff and Henry Wace, vol. 5, *Gregory of Nyssa: Dogmatic Treatises, Etc.* (New York: Christian Literature, 1983), 334.

rule. R. B. Jamieson and Tyler R. Wittman are helpful in this regard when they write, "Scripture sometimes attributes to only one divine person a perfection, action, or name common to all three, because of some contextual fit or analogy between the common attribute and the divine person in question. *Read such passages in a way that does not compromise the Trinity's essential oneness and equality.*"[10]

The Divine Will and the Divine Decree

The early church fathers have taught us that since God's power is one, God's will must be one, and if God's will is one, the operations of that one will must also be one. But how are we to understand this emphasis on singularity in light of the seemingly *many distinct* actions attributed to Father, Son, and Spirit in the Scriptures? As we have seen throughout this book, we will have a hard time answering this question without the conceptual distinction between *theologia* and *oikonomia*—theology and economy, who God *is* and what God *does*. In terms of God's life *ad intra*—that is, who God is in himself— the will of God is one with God himself. This is because (as we saw in chapter 5) God is *simple* and is therefore not composed of any parts. Simplicity excludes any kind of composition, including the composition of God's *being* and God's *will*. In other words, God's will is not separable from God's being. Thus, in the words of the post-Reformation scholastic, Petrus van Mastricht, "The will of God is most simple because it is the willing God himself."[11] That is

---

[10] R. B. Jamieson and Tyler R. Wittman, *Biblical Reasoning: Christological and Trinitarian Rules for Exegesis* (Grand Rapids: 2022), 106, emphasis added.

[11] Peter van Mastricht, *Theoretical-Practical Theology,* vol. 2, *Faith in the Triune God,* ed. Joel R. Beeke (Grand Rapids: Reformation Heritage Books, 2019), 2:15.X.

God's will *ad intra*, and it means that nothing exists *at all* outside of his will.

What about God's works *ad extra?* That is, what does God's will look like in view of the *oikonomia*—the economy? What does the timelessly eternal divine will look like in relation to everything that is not God? The broad, catch-all category we give for this *ad extra* manifestation of God's *ad intra* will is "the divine decree." Chapter 3 of the Second London Baptist Confession of Faith (1689), on "God's Decree," describes this crucial concept:

> God hath Decreed in himself from all Eternity, by the most wise and holy Counsel of his own will, freely and unchangeably, all things whatsoever comes to pass; yet so as thereby is God neither the author of sin, nor hath fellowship with any therein, nor is violence offered to the will of the Creature, nor yet is the liberty, or contingency of second causes taken away, but rather established, in which appears his wisdom in disposing all things, and power, and faithfulness, in accomplishing his Decree.[12]

Everything that is not God is a manifestation of God's divine decree. In his commentary on the Second London Baptist Confession, James M. Renihan writes, "The eternal decree is accomplished in the created realm. Everything that happens external to God is the realization of His holy will."[13] This does not mean that all things in creation collapse into one another, but it does mean that all things that exist in creation are finite expressions of God's infinite will.

---

[12] The Second London Baptist Confession of Faith, par. 3.1.

[13] James M. Renihan, *To the Judicious and Impartial Reader: A Contextual-Historical Exposition of the Second London Baptist Confession of Faith, Baptist Symbolics*, vol. 2 (Cape Coral, FL: Founders, 2022), 108.

Again, Mastricht is instructive for us when he says, "The will of God is one and only one, yet it is distinguished by us into various modes, first on account of the different kinds of things that it wills, next on account of the different modes in which we see that it wills what it wills."[14]

All this helps us to better grasp how we can simultaneously maintain the singularity of the Trinity's will and operations while also distinguishing various works that God accomplishes in the economy. The works of creation, providence, redemption, and glorification are distinct for us who live in their temporal structure, but they are all expressions of the singular divine decree, which is the expression of the single divine will, which we attribute to the single divine essence of the Father, Son, and Spirit.[15]

Divine Appropriations: Inseparable Operations' Doctrinal Corollary

To attribute the work of salvation to the Trinity in general seems fair enough, but does that mean that the Father, Son, and Spirit must have all equally become incarnate? Thomas Aquinas actually entertained this very question in his *Summa Theologia*: "Whether One Person Without Another Can Assume a Created Nature?" In his typical fashion, Aquinas brings up several possible objections to the answer he proposes. The first objection he offers is the doctrine

---

[14] Mastricht, *Theoretical-Practical Theology*, 2:15.XXII.

[15] For this reason, Francis Turretin says that God's decrees "do not differ really from his essence, since the will of God (with which they are identified) is nothing else than the essence itself willing . . ." Therefore, he can describe the decree as immanent and intrinsic, though that which God decrees takes effect in creation, which is extrinsic. Francis Turretin, *Institutes of Elenctic Theology*, vol. 1 (Phillipsburg: P&R, 1992), 1:312.

of inseparable operations: "It would seem that one Person cannot assume a created nature without another assuming it. For *the works of the Trinity are inseparable,* as Augustine says . . . But as the three Persons have one essence, so likewise They have one operation. Now to assume [a human nature] is an operation. Therefore it cannot belong to one without belonging to another."[16]

Do you see the dilemma we have created for ourselves? If the doctrine of inseparable operations is true and if the incarnation is an action inseparably carried out by the undivided Trinity, we might well imagine this means every member of the Trinity took on flesh! Yet such a teaching is patently contrary to the teaching of Scripture.

How does Aquinas get out of this pickle? He does what he does so well: he distinguishes. Specifically, he distinguishes the two things an "assumption" implies: "the *act of* assuming and *the term* of assumption."[17] Regarding the "act of assumption," Aquinas acknowledges, in agreement with the principle of inseparable operations, that the "act of assumption proceeds from the divine power, which is common to the three Persons."[18] In other words, the incarnation is a *triune act*—an operation inseparably carried out by all three persons. Father, Son, and Spirit bring about the miracle of the incarnation since every work of God is the one, single act of the Holy Trinity. But regarding the other part of assumption, namely "the term of assumption," Aquinas writes, "the term of the assumption is a Person . . . Hence what has to do with action in the assumption is common to the three Persons; but what pertains to the nature of term [assumption] belongs to one Person in such a

---

[16] Aquinas, *Summa Theologiae,* vol. 48, *The Incarnate Word,* 3a. 1–6 (Cambridge: Cambridge University Press, 2006), 3a.3.4.

[17] Aquinas, 3a.3.4.

[18] Aquinas, 3a.3.4.

manner as not to belong to another."[19] Therefore, the Son—not the Father, nor the Spirit—assumed a human nature.

In this way, Aquinas makes a crucial distinction between the power that carries out an action and the divine person on whom such an action *terminates* in the economy. The inseparable operation of the incarnation terminates on the divine person of the Son when he assumes a human nature in the economy of salvation history. This "termination" helps us understand *divine appropriations*. Gilles Emery defines divine appropriations in this way: the New Testament "frequently attributes an action or an effect to a divine person in a special way, without excluding the two others."[20] The Nicene Creed is a fine example of appropriations. The creed can attribute an action or an attribute to a person of the Trinity. It can say, for instance, that the Father is "almighty" or all governing over creation. Or it can say that the Spirit is "Holy." Yet there are not three almighties but one Almighty (as the Athanasian Creed says). Likewise, no one person of the Trinity is less "holy" than another.

What, then, is the *logic* of divine appropriations? Are they entirely arbitrary? Again, consider the incarnation: would it be just as fitting if *Mediator* were appropriated to the Father so that he is the one who is sent by the Son to become incarnate for the sake of accomplishing the mission of redemption? Was it more fitting if he had prayed, "My Son, please take this cup from me; nevertheless, not my will but your will be done"?[21] Or would it be

---

[19] Aquinas, 3a.3.4.

[20] Gilles Emery, *The Trinity: An Introduction to Catholic Doctrine on the Triune God* (Washington, DC: Catholic University of America Press, 2011), 165.

[21] Also, Aquinas explains that it is so fitting for the Son to become man because as the Word he is the Exemplar for all creation (*ST* 3a.3.8). He is following John of Damascus.

just as fitting to appropriate *Helper* to the Son so that he is poured out on the church at Pentecost rather than the Spirit? The answer to all these questions is *no*.[22] Divine appropriations are always a *fitting* correspondence to the eternal relations of the Trinity *ad intra*. *This point is crucial.* Throughout this book, we have endeavored to distinguish between *essential* properties (that which the Father, Son, and Spirit share wholly by virtue of their common, simple essence) and *personal* properties (that which distinguishes Father, Son, and Spirit from one another). We could say, therefore, that the doctrine of inseparable operations corresponds to the *essential properties*, whereas the doctrine of divine appropriations corresponds to *personal properties*. So, for example, the outpouring of the Spirit at Pentecost is a divine operation and is therefore carried out by the Father, Son, and Spirit, who are one in essence and will. Nevertheless, the Nicene Creed is right to appropriate the title "Life-Giver," since such an outpouring *terminates* on the Spirit and not on the Father or the Son.[23] Why? Because such a

---

[22] To qualify, we do not deny that the *power* to assume a human nature belongs to all three persons since they have the one essence (and therefore, power) in common. Our point is only that it is *fitting* that the Son is made flesh. See Aquinas, *ST* 3a. 3.5.

[23] Although an extended discussion on the distinction would take us too far beyond the scope of our present concerns, we should note that divine appropriations and trinitarian missions are not synonyms. For instance, Scripture may appropriate the title *Redeemer* to the Son in eternity since Ephesians 1 says we have been chosen in Christ before the foundation of the world (v. 4). However, when we refer to the mission of the Son, we are referring to the Father's sending the Son to become incarnate in history for the sake of our redemption. All that to say, one of the conceptual distinctions between appropriation and mission has to do with *time*. As Aquinas says, "Mission signifies not only procession from the principle, but also determines the temporal term of the procession. Hence mission is only temporal. Or we may say that it includes

termination *fittingly corresponds* to the Spirit's procession from the Father and the Son. The outpouring of the Spirit at Pentecost, in other words, is a fitting expression of the Spirit's *personal property*. All this is why, when we read about the persons of the Trinity acting in various ways in the Scriptures, we should "learn to count persons rather than actions."[24]

Consider the example of the incarnation. As mentioned before, the life of Christ seems, at first glance, to pose a problem for this doctrine of inseparable operations. Does the scene in the garden of Gethsemane not depict the *Son's* actions (i.e., begging for the Father to take his cup) as set over and against the *Father's* action (i.e., refusing the Son's request) (Matt 26:39)?

There are two truths we must keep in mind with passages like these. First, we must remember that nothing we see Christ doing in the Gospels falls outside the context of the hypostatic union. This means that everything Christ does before our eyes he does as the God-*man,* whose humanity is true and whole and perfect. As the God-man, the person of the Son not only subsists in the divine nature but in a human nature. It follows, therefore, that he has both a divine will (which is the one will of the Trinity) as well as a human will. This means that the *will* Christ lays before the Father is not the divine will he has as an essential divine property (which

---

the eternal procession, with the addition of a temporal effect." Thomas Aquinas, *Summa Theologiae*, vol. 7, *Father, Son and Holy Ghost*, 1a 33-43 (Cambridge: Cambridge University Press, 2006), 1a.43.2. Divine appropriations, on the other hand, refers to how a divine perfection or a divine work may be attributed to a person, though never to the exclusion of the other persons (see Emery's definition given previously). For more on divine missions, see Adonis Vidu, *Divine Missions: An Introduction* (Eugene, OR: Cascade Books, 2021).

[24] Jamieson and Wittman, *Biblical Reasoning*, 106.

is the Father's will, since there is only one divine will) but is rather his human will. This act of obedience to fulfill all righteousness is an act rendered with the human will of a human nature on behalf of *human beings*. Keeping this in mind brings much conceptual clarity to the many examples we find in the Gospels that seem to contradict inseparable operations. The tension we feel in Gethsemane is real, otherwise we might doubt whether Christ truly was made flesh. Yet it is not the tension between two separable, divisible divine operations, as if there were multiple divine wills in the Trinity. Rather, says Maximus the Confessor, the garden results in a "perfect harmony"—"not my will, but yours, be done" (Luke 22:42).[25] For he who is the most perfect man offers the costliest act of humiliation to God in the face of unspeakable suffering. Christ is not *divided*. As the Chalcedonian Definition reads, the hypostatic union concurs "into a single person and a single subsistent being; he is not parted or divided into two persons, but one and the same only-begotten Son, God, Word, Lord Jesus Christ."[26] We are still seeing a *divine person* act in that concession of obedience in the garden.

Second, the incarnation is not the solo performance we might have thought it was at first glance.[27] Everything in the Gospels must necessarily be understood as the *Trinity's* work of redemption, inseparably connected to the rest of the incarnation—which includes not only Christ's conception but also his life of miracles, his transfiguration, his death on the cross, his descent to Hades,

---

[25] Maximus the Confessor, *Opusculum 6*, in *The Cosmic Mystery of Christ* (New York: St Vladimir's Seminary Press, 2003), 174.

[26] Van Dixhoorn, *Creeds*, 27

[27] See Michael Allen, *Grounded in Heaven: Recentering Christian Hope and Life on God* (Downers Grove, IL: Eerdmans, 2018), 78.

his resurrection, and his ascension.[28] The entire "moment" of the incarnation is carried out by the Trinity: it is the event of the Father sending (Rom 8:3), the Son coming to take on flesh (John 1:14), and the Spirit miraculously conceiving (Luke 1:35). These are not three separate actions by three separate wills. Everything God does is *from* the Father, *through* the Son, and *in* the Spirit. God sent, God came, and God effected, and "each verb names the same single act of incarnation."[29]

Communion with the Holy Trinity

The payoff of inseparable operations is clear in terms of appropriate Bible reading and trinitarian doctrine. Keeping this central truth in mind protects us from thinking unbecoming thoughts about our triune God. But what does this mean for our *worship* of the Trinity? Even further, what does this mean for our *communion* with the Trinity?

The great Puritan pastor John Owen was a staunch defender of trinitarian orthodoxy, and therefore, he affirmed the doctrine of inseparable operations. Yet he wrote an entire book on communion with the Trinity, wherein he argues for and defends the Christian practice of communing with each person *distinctly*. How does he frame this practice conceptually? Right at the interplay between inseparable operations and divine appropriations! Owen writes:

> Now, the works that outwardly are of God (called "Trinitatis ad extra"), which are commonly said to be *common and undivided*, are either wholly so, and in all respects, as all

---

[28] See Dominic Legge, *The Trinitarian Christology of St. Thomas Aquinas* (Oxford: Oxford University Press, 2021).

[29] Jamieson and Wittman, *Biblical Reasoning*, 122.

works of common providence; or else, being common in respect of their acts, they are distinguished in respect of that principle, or next and immediate rise in the manner of operation: so creation is *appropriated* to the Father, redemption to the Son.[30]

Owen is careful to insist on worshipping God as Trinity. We ought never render *worship* to one person in isolation from the other, as if each were worthy of different degrees of glory. The "prime *object* of divine worship," for Owen, is "the nature or essence of God."[31] However, Owen also considers divine appropriations an accommodation of sorts—God intends divine appropriations to inform and aid us in our prayer and fellowship with the Trinity. In this way, both inseparable operations and divine appropriations bring shape to our praise. So, Owen can say, on the one hand, "There is a concurrence of the *actings* and operations of the whole Deity in that *dispensation*, wherein each person concurs to the work of our salvation, unto every *act* of our communion with each singular person. . . . By whatsoever act we hold communion with any person, there is an *influence* from every person to the putting forth of that act."[32] In other words, inseparable operations should chasten our conception of fellowship with the Trinity. As we commune with one person, we ought not imagine that the other two are in any way separable.

But this does not preclude him from saying, on the other hand, that "the saints have distinct communion with the Father, and the Son, and the Holy Spirit (that is, distinctly with the Father, and distinctly with the Son, and distinctly with the Holy

---

[30] John Owen, *The Works of John Owen*, ed. William Gould (repr., Edinburgh: Banner of Truth Trust, 2009), 2:18.

[31] Owen, 2:18; italics in the original.

[32] Owen, 2:18; italics in the original.

Spirit)."[33] According to Owen, the history of redemption should inform the way this prayerful communion takes place. We enjoy communion with the Father as the boundless source of all divine love—the reservoir we have entered into by our spiritual adoption. Our entire salvation is an outflow of his loving care. But how was his love manifested to us? It was manifested to us by the arrival of the Son—our elder Brother, our Bridegroom, our Good Shepherd. His expression of divine love in living, dying, rising, and ascending for us is the grace through which we receive the love of God the Father. Apart from his gracious mediation, we would know nothing of the Father's love. But how were we united to Christ? How did we come to share in his atoning, mediating work? The Spirit of the Father and the Son *baptized* us into Christ. In effect, we receive the Spirit's consolation and comfort in Christ. All of this is to describe the Trinity's inseparable operation of redemption, yet this operation was carried out before our eyes through various divine appropriations. Appropriations, therefore, should inform the way we commune with God at the personal level.

Likewise, consider the triune God to whom Christians pray. The act of prayer is made possible only because we have been welcomed into the life of the Trinity in salvation. When we pray, we can look down, as it were, at the foundation of our activity and reason in a catechetical manner along these lines:

Q. Who is this Father to whom I pray?
A. He is the unbegotten Father of his Son and Spirit.

Q. How do I imagine I have the right to pray to such a one?
A. Because I pray in the name of Christ by the power of the Spirit—the Spirit has united me to Christ and has

---

[33] Owen, 2:9.

given me the desire to pray. I pray to the Father because I have a powerful elder Brother who has invited me to receive the love of the Father.

Q. How did I come to cling to this Christ by faith?
A. *The Spirit of God removed Satan's veil, and I saw Christ in all his beauty, and I could not do otherwise* (cf., 2 Cor 3:12–4:6).

At the close of each of those questions, we should find an endless supply of gratitude and fodder for communion. It is fitting for us to thank *the Father* for his endless love to create us and draw us into his paternal affection. We should thank *the Son* for being our Good Shepherd and laying his life down for us so that we may receive his grace. We ought to render thanks to *the Spirit* for pouring God's love into our hearts, for being our consolation and Comforter, and for uniting us to Christ and all his blessings. And in doing so, we should offer worship to the Father, Son, and Spirit, who is one God, world without end. Amen.

The Beatific Vision: The Sight of Triune Beauty

The ultimate manifestation of this communion is what awaits every believer in the beatific vision—the blessed hope of seeing God. This hope has fallen into obscurity in many evangelical quarters, but it is difficult to exaggerate its centrality to the Christian faith, as exemplified by most Christians across the great tradition. This "happy vision" or "blessed vision" is the blessed hope of beholding God in heaven, and it is the telos of the human soul. The beatific vision is what Moses was impatient to see on Mount Horeb (cf., Exod 33:18–23), and it has been the blessed hope of the vast majority of saints down through the centuries. This doctrine is what animated the prayers and contemplations of so many wonderful theologians like Gregory of Nyssa, Augustine, Anselm of Canterbury, Thomas Aquinas, John Calvin, John Owen, and countless more. According to these thinkers, the beatific vision is the central, animating hope of the Christian soul, and it is the telos of every desire. All roads of desire lead here. Christians of the past had good reason to believe this, of course. After all, the promise of the beatific vision allures and draws the very biblical authors themselves, from Moses (Exod 33:18–23) to David (Ps 27:4), from Job (Job 19:26) to Isaiah (Isa 24:23), from Paul (1 Cor 13:13) to John (1 John 3:2). Consider these biblical examples from the Psalter.

One of the features of modern exegesis is a deep and abiding concern for *context* and the human biblical author's authorial intent. To be sure, this due respect and attention to such a major literary facet of the text has yielded treasures that we should not dismiss lightly. However, this level of concern, detached from canonical and theological (and even philosophical) questions has its limitations. Not all theological insights to be found in any given text are gleanable from asking and answering historical questions surrounding the passage's context. Psalm 17:15 provides a good example to illustrate the limitations of such a constrained exegesis.

David's prayer in Psalm 17 is, in many ways, unremarkable for its kind. Like many of David's psalms, it is a cry for help to God alone. According to David, he is wrongfully pursued by "deadly enemies" (v. 9). These enemies "advance against" David and "are determined to throw [him] to the ground" (v. 11). The chief enemy is "like a lion eager to tear" (v. 12), and so David appeals to God—who is sovereign over even the very life of his oppressors (v. 14)—to "hear a just cause" (v. 1). The text itself does not provide with certainty the occasion for this psalm, but David had his fair share of enemies, and it is not difficult to imagine he wrote it under the duress of being hunted by any one of them (Saul particularly stands out as a believable candidate for the "lion" David refers to here (cf. 1 Sam 19–31).

In this context, then, verse 15 seems to commend itself as David's consolation of confidence in God to answer his prayer: "But I will see your face in righteousness; when I awake, I will be satisfied with your presence" (Ps 17:15). There seems to be some ambiguity as to whether David means to say that he will behold God's face in his (David's) own righteousness (as vv. 2 and 3 might seem to suggest) or behold God's face in *God's* righteousness (as the parallel of v. 15b might suggest—"in righteousness," corresponds to "*your* likeness"). It may be that both are in view, but which aspect receives primary punctuation will depend on how one answers the most relevant question with respect to our purposes here: Does David refer merely to consolation he will receive in this life, or does he refer to something else as well? David will behold God's face in righteousness and will be satisfied with God's likeness, *when he wakes*. When is that? Does David speak of the morning following this prayer, or does he refer to waking from the sleep of death in the resurrection? If our hermeneutical concerns are constrained merely to describe what is happening in David's historical context at the time of the origin of Psalm 17, we would be hard-pressed to squeeze a whole doctrine of the resurrection and the beatific vision into such a small phrase. Such constraint is precisely why many biblical commentators are so reluctant to describe anything beyond David's confidence in his deliverance from *this particular* peril. For example, Rolf Jacobson and Beth Tanner modestly conclude their comments on Psalm 17:15 in this way, "The psalmist, having prayed himself as it were almost into an exhausted sleep, closes his eyes in the trusting confidence that the new day will dawn with hope—because all tomorrows are in the hands of the Lord."[34] Likewise, Derek Kidner observes how "some expositors suggest that the words *when I awake* meant to the psalmist no more than this," namely, that David was confident in God's vindication of his own righteousness.[35]

If, however, we allow ourselves to read Ps 17:15 not merely in light of the historical occasion for the prayer but also in light of what David has written elsewhere, and indeed, what all the biblical authors have written, such a minimal interpretation of "when I awake" does not satisfy. This is the very same David, after all, who penned Ps 27:4. This psalm is written in a similar context to that of Psalm 17, with a similar tone—David can remain undaunted by his "evildoers," who "came against" him to "devour [his] flesh" (Ps 27:2), because "the LORD is [his] light and [his] salvation" (v. 1). In this context, David expresses his single-minded desire: "I have asked one thing from the LORD; it is what I desire: to dwell in the house of the LORD all the days of my life, gazing on the beauty of the LORD and seeking him in his temple" (v. 4). That David is speaking of a desire that by necessity points beyond this life is evident from the fact that he already takes comfort in God as his light and his salvation. He is already within the "stronghold of [his] life" (v. 1), yet despite the hopeful and glorious reality he enjoys as he writes these words, he longs for something *more*. Like Moses, who enjoyed previously unparalleled access to God's presence, he was so bold as to ask—single-mindedly—for something else. David does not simply pine after a life of contemplation in the

---

[34] Rolf A. Jacobson and Beth LaNeel Tanner, "Book One of the Psalter: Psalms 1–41," in *The Book of Psalms*, ed. Nancy deClaissé-Walford, Rolf A. Jacobson, and Beth LaNeel Tanner (Grand Rapids: Eerdmans, 2014), 189.

[35] Derek Kidner, *Psalms 1–72: An Introduction and Commentary* (Downers Grove, IL: InterVarsity, 1973), 107.

Lord's temple in Jerusalem (indeed, he *could not* long for this, since the temple in Jerusalem would not be built in his lifetime); he longs to dwell in *the Lord's true house*, where he can see not merely the beauty of the temple but the beauty of the Lord himself. To "[gaze] on the beauty of the LORD" is the "one thing" for which he asks (v. 4).

The singularity of this request, of course, does not bespeak an absolute unwillingness to request anything else of God. Instead, we should understand this desire—the desire to "gaze upon the beauty of the LORD"—as the desire that subsumes all other desires. All other legitimate requests of the Lord eventuate in this one. All answered prayers, for David, find their ultimate answer in being in the house of the Lord, gazing upon his beauty. Such a pure expression of desire for God—such an unveiled and revelatory moment of deep sincerity—accords with what we find in other passages, such as Exod 33:18; Isa 33:17; 1 Cor 13:9–11; and Rev 22:3–5.

We must conclude, therefore, that whatever David means by "awake" in Ps 17:15, the verse cannot *merely* signify David's assurance of waking the next day, content with God in the face of opposition. To be sure, the text can certainly refer *at least* to such an immediate hope, but surely Ps 17:15 calls our mind to a hope that transcends this age and this life. "The sight of God is either by faith on earth," writes the nineteenth-century biblical commentator, William S. Plumer, "or by vision in heaven. Beholding as by a glass darkly the glory of the Lord on earth is a pledge of beholding his glory in the visions of immortality."[36] Plumer rightly indicates that both readings are legitimate, depending on which horizon is

---

[36] William S. Plumer, *Psalms: A Critical and Expository Commentary with Doctrinal and Practical Remarks* (Edinburgh: Banner of Truth Trust, 1975; repr., 1978), 228.

in view: communion with God before or after the resurrection. Plumer writes:

> Beholding as by a glass darkly the glory of the Lord on earth is a pledge of beholding his glory in the visions of immortality. I shall be satisfied with thy likeness, *when I wake* either every morning, and find myself with God, enjoying his favor and friendship, and so beholding him in his works of providence and grace; or as when one awakes from sleep, the emblem of death, I shall be delivered from these impending evils, and shall thus be assured of thy love; or above all, when I awake from my last sleep of death and in the glories of a resurrection state I shall see God face to face, then my discoveries of him shall bring everlasting satisfaction to my soul.[37]

In the psalms, David finds deep consolation in God's deliverance from temporal danger. But what becomes clear in consideration of all his reflections—and in light of the biblical canon as a whole—is that David's deepest consolation is the blessed hope of the beatific vision. Some of the most affective lines in all the psalter—like those in Ps 17:15 or Ps 27:4—point the reader beyond the temporal circumstances of David the king or David the politician to the heavenly hope of David the *worshipper*. Like rays of transcendent light cutting through the firmament and clouds of transient struggles, David evinces a heart that is beckoned beyond earth's atmosphere into the highest heavens. His otherworldly hope is in the blessed vision—the hope to behold and be satisfied by the face and likeness of him who *is* righteousness (Ps 17:15), the hope to

---

[37] Plumer, *Psalms*, 228.

dwell in the house of the Lord to *gaze* upon his beauty (Ps 27:4)—which is a hope that is biblically well-founded.

So, the beatific vision is clearly a biblical hope. But in recent history, much scholarly attention has been given to debates surrounding the particulars of the beatific vision. Will this sight be purely *ocular*, or will it be *intellectual*? Will believers be glorified *by* the beatific vision, or will the beatific vision *cause* glorification? While a full engagement with all these questions is beyond the immediate scope of the present book, it is worthwhile to close our reflections by considering how the doctrine of inseparable operations paves a way to navigating one important and debated question surrounding the beatific vision: will we behold the human nature of *Christ*, or will we behold the *essence* of God?[38] If we hold inseparable operations for all its worth, we can answer this either/or question with a *yes*. Michael Allen is helpful when he writes:

> The attendant condition of the humanity of Christ does not mean that the blessed vision of God in the face of Christ can be reduced to a vision of his humanity. Rather, we see him: the person of the Son of God, "God of God, Light of Light, Very God of Very God." . . . The Son as Son is visible. But the Son as Son is visible by means of his humanity.[39]

In Christ, therefore, "we see *God* and not simply an instrument of or attachment to God in this vision."[40] God's ultimate self-revelation

---

[38] For a thorough engagement of this doctrine, along with adjudications of these and other debated questions, see Samuel G. Parkison, *To Gaze upon God: The Beatific Vision in Doctrine, Tradition, and Practice* (Downers Grove, IL: IVP Academic, 2024).

[39] Allen, *Grounded in Heaven*, 79.

[40] Allen, 80.

in the beatific vision, in that world of love where our glorified bodies will be fit for the kind of ecstasy of which we can only *dream* at present, will be an external work of the Trinity and will therefore be one. This is the highest goal, the greatest good, and the chiefest delight of the soul. And because of the inseparable operations of the Trinity to redeem us, it is an unshakeable promise for those of us who are in Christ. We shall see God, and we shall delight in him in increasing measure forever and ever.

> *Glory be to the Father*
> *and to the Son*
> *and to the Holy Spirit.*
> *As it was in the beginning,*
> *is now,*
> *and ever shall be,*
> *world without end.*
> *Amen.*[41]

---

[41] Gloria Patri. See Jonathan Gibson, *Be Thou My Vision* (Wheaton, IL: Crossway, 2021), 41.

CONCLUSION

In one of the more influential books written on the Trinity, the church father Augustine of Hippo wrote, "For this is the fullness of our joy, than which there is nothing greater: to enjoy God the Trinity in whose image we have been made."[1] Augustine's view of God's triunity was not reserved for those who pursue theological vocation; it was not a doctrine reserved for academia; it was not a mere abstraction that bore no meaning in the normal rhythms of the Christian life. Instead, for Augustine, the Trinity was the highest form of enjoyment in this life and the next. The book you hold in your hands should be thought of as nothing other than a six-chapter reflection in agreement with the North African bishop. The authors of this book agree with those words written roughly 1,600 hundred years ago: the triune God—who is Father, Son, and Spirit—is the fullness of our joy.

We believe that the Trinity is the source, the substance, and the ultimate goal of the Christian life. All things, seen and unseen, come *from* the Trinity, are substantiated and preserved *by* the Trinity, and will one day—whether in glorious union or terrifying

---

[1] Augustine, *The Trinity*, ed. H. Dressler, trans. S. McKenna (Washington, DC: Catholic University of America Press, 1963), 26.

judgment—return *to* the Trinity. In this way, there is a sort of disorder when asking the question, "How does the doctrine of the Trinity impact my Christian life?" What we hope has become clear from the pages of this book is that the Trinity is not a doctrine to be somewhat applied to piety; rather, all things in the Christian life find their meaning and fulfillment in light of the Trinity. The Trinity is not another doctrine within the Christian faith; the Trinity is the Christian faith in so much as all things ought to be rooted in their proper principle—participate in the triune life of God. There is no good gift we possess that we did not receive from the triune God, and there is no trial in this life through which the Holy Trinity cannot sustain us.

As Paul says in Acts 17, it is in the triune God that "we live and move and have our being" (v. 28). This again shows the disordered thinking that seeks to draw out mere practical points of piety from the doctrine of the Trinity. It is not the case that the Trinity *may* impact the way you live. Rather, you live *because* of the Trinity. The Trinity is as essential a doctrine as oxygen is an element; without either, you would perish.

The glorious task of contemplating Christian theology should be seen as a deep well of joy. For in the task of thinking Christianly, our minds may retreat to those glorious topics of creation, salvation, the church, and so much more. However, these subjects of Christian theology are living on borrowed glory, for they derive their splendor from their relation to the triune God. Indeed, to study the doctrine of creation is to contemplate *the Trinity's* handiwork; to study the doctrine of salvation is to contemplate *the Trinity's* redemption of an unworthy people; to study the doctrine of the church is to contemplate *the Trinity's* elect people in relation to one another. Each field of Christian thought is rooted in and derivative of that first and most important principle of Christian thinking—God himself.

In his work on Christian theology, the eighteenth-century Baptist theologian, John Gill, captured well the way the Trinity gloriously permeates all that is the Christian life, writing: "The doctrine of the Trinity is often represented as a speculative point, of no great moment whether it is believed or no, too mysterious and curious to be pried into, and that it had better be let alone than meddled with; but alas! it enters into the whole of our salvation, and all parts of it; into all the doctrines of the gospel, and into the experience of the saints; there is no doing without it."[2] Gill is correct to suggest that the Trinity—even with all its mystery intact—enters into all parts of our lives. The Christian religion is a trinitarian faith through and through.

It is with this recognition in hand, one that has hopefully become clear through this project, that all the people of the world belong to the Trinity, and the doctrine of the Trinity is for all people. We ought to come to a confession in the conclusion of this book: our confession is that we have not really said anything overly brilliant in these pages. Nothing in this book is new per se; nothing in this book ought to be strikingly original. No, instead of innovation we have pursued *rediscovery and retrieval*. We have aimed to bring a doctrine found in the Scriptures and codified by the ancient church into the hands of today's believing community. Our greatest goal with these pages is that normal believers, who find themselves in normal churches, with normal lives, and normal Christian imaginations, would find themselves enthralled by the triune God.

Our hope is that both believers individually and churches corporately would see the Trinity as the supreme source of life and

---

[2] John Gill, *A Complete Body of Doctrinal and Practical Divinity* (Paris, AR: The Baptist Standard Bearer, 2007), 138.

joy, for an understanding of the Trinity shaped by the Bible and the church of *yesterday* has much to say *today*. In whatever way what we have said thus far in the book can said to be "classical," we hope it does not remain "classic," as if it is reserved for those who *have* lived. Rather, we hope a "classical" understanding of the Trinity will galvanize today's church to take the whole counsel of God, along with the church's historic confession, seriously, bending the life of the contemporary church in this direction. We believe the church's mission, purpose, confession, participation, communion, worship, and the like ought all to have a trinitarian shape. As theology seeks first and foremost to contemplate the triune God and by derivation everything else in relation to God, we believe every Christian should ask how each corner of his or her Christian life is shaped by the triune God.

Finally, we believe that the Trinity is not only the source and substance of *this* life but also the life to come. As Paul wrote to the Corinthian church, "We all, with unveiled faces, are looking as in a mirror at the glory of the Lord and are being transformed into the same image from glory to glory" (2 Cor 3:18). The primary concern of the Christian in this life is to behold God in the ways appropriate to our creatureliness—that is, in the Scripture, with God's people, for God's glory. Yet one day the church's faith will become sight, and instead of seeing God "as in a mirror" we will one day see him "face to face." Again, as the apostle Paul wrote, "For now we see only a reflection as in a mirror, but then face to face. Now I know in part, but then I will know fully, as I am fully known" (1 Cor 13:12).

Whereas in the here and now we have only seen the triune God as a reflection in a mirror or with a veiled face, we will one day behold his glory evermore in the beatific vision. In this way, attempting to behold the triune God in this life is but a small, preparatory participation in our eternal vocation. One day we will lay hold of the vision which beatifies, and the deepest longings of our redeemed soul will be met in the sight of the Almighty. But Christian, this is not yet our story. The vision of God that will satisfy our soul still resides in the "not yet" of our "already-not yet" life, and until the two collide as Jesus comes back to judge the living and the dead, we strive to continually turn our mind's eye Godward.

Therefore, with all that we are, may we do the important work—both individually and corporately—to behold our triune God. May we continue to be a people of the Book and search the Scriptures for the eternally unbegotten Father, the eternally generated Son, and the eternally spirated Holy Spirit. Until our faith is sight, may we hold fast to the confession that we have received and continue to proclaim with the history of the church:[3]

> I believe in one God, the Father Almighty,
>   Maker of heaven and earth, and
>   of all things visible and invisible.
>
> And in one Lord Jesus Christ, the only-begotten Son of God,
>   begotten of the Father before all worlds;
>   God of God, Light of Light,
>   very God of very God;
>   begotten, not made,
>   being of the one substance with the Father,
>   by whom all things were made.
>   Who, for us men and for our salvation,
>   came down from heaven
>   and was incarnate by the Holy Spirit of the Virgin Mary,

---

[3] Chad Van Dixhoorn, *Creeds, Confessions, and Catechisms: A Reader's Edition* (Wheaton, IL: Crossway, 2022), 17.

and was made man;
and was crucified also for us under Pontius Pilate;
he suffered and was buried;
and the third day he rose again, according to the Scriptures;
and ascended into heaven,
and sits on the right hand of the Father;
and he shall come again, with glory,
to judge the living and the dead;
whose kingdom shall have no end.

And I believe in the Holy Spirit,
the Lord and Giver of life;
who proceeds from the Father and the Son;
who with the Father and the Son together is worshiped and glorified;
who spoke by the prophets.
And I believe in one holy catholic and apostolic church.
I acknowledge one baptism for the remission of sins;
and I look for the resurrection of the dead,
and the life of the world to come. Amen.

APPENDIX: THE CREEDS IN THE LIFE OF THE CHURCH

Of the many themes and emphases in this book, one of the more consistent threads throughout is the gift that is the history of the church, or what we sometimes call the great tradition. As modern Christians, we have inherited the gift of a centuries-old conversation about God and all things in relation to him. The history of the church's conversation about our triune God contains those moments in which the church confessed the faith once and for all delivered to the saints not only through orations and homilies but also through writing, as the church put on paper her codified notions of God and his glory. We, the authors of this book, find immense value in retrieving the conciliar and codified witness of church history through creeds and confessions of the past as a clear and faithful witness to classical trinitarianism.

As should be evident from the preceding material, we do not find the church's historic creeds and confessions to have the same kind of authority as God's inspired Word—the Holy Scripture. Rather, we see the authority of the creeds and confessions as a *derivative* authority. The historic confessions of the church have authority because they are accurate accounts of the biblical data and therefore carry an authority as instruments in the hands of the church for discipline and discipleship. By participating in the creedal affirmation of the church, we align ourselves with those who have gone before us in hopes of preserving the faith once and for all delivered to the saints.

More than mere *historical* artifacts, we believe that these documents have living meaning for today's church. To this end, we hope to serve readers by mentioning three benefits of the historic creeds, concluding with an additional example of potential ways of incorporating the creeds into the church's liturgical rhythms.[1]

To Glorify God by Guarding Sound Doctrine

The health of our confession is a biblical concern. For example, one mark of Christian maturity is that one's "senses have been trained to distinguish between good from evil" (Heb 5:14 ESV). Moreover, the apostle Paul tells Timothy to stand firm on the traditions he was taught and to watch his life and doctrine (1 Tim 1:18–19; 4:16). Elsewhere, he tells Titus that one qualification of an elder is that he hold firm to the trustworthy Word so that he may instruct in sound doctrine and rebuke those who oppose it (Titus 1:9).

As seen in the early church's trinitarian and Christological controversies, a mere collection of Bible quotations and citations does not distinguish truth from falsehood. At Nicaea, for example, those who affirmed Christ's eternal divine nature and those who opposed it both came prepared with their biblical passages.

---

[1] For similar and further benefits of the creeds in the life of the church, see J. V. Fesko, *The Need for Creeds Today: Confessional Faith in a Faithless Age* (Grand Rapids: Baker Academic, 2020), 77–96; Carl R. Trueman, *The Creedal Imperative* (Wheaton, IL: Crossway, 2012), 159–85.

Therefore, a healthy creed from the church will take not only biblical *reading* but also biblical *reasoning*. As a rule of faith, the creeds serve as guardrails for Christians while they seek to contemplate the variegated principles laid down in the scriptural data. With this point is the double blessing of (1) guarding our reading of God's Word and (2) identifying and guarding against those who might seek to manipulate or malign that very Word. Creeds enable the church by establishing and cultivating both her doctrinal being (*esse*) and her well-being (*bene esse*).[2]

To Maintain Unity

A church that confesses, "There is one true God who eternally exists as Father, Son, and Spirit" or that the only begotten Son came "for us and for our salvation," signals herself as distinct and excludes all other religions. Christians who have these codified expressions in their lives demonstrate that they are not members of a novel movement but find themselves within a communion of saints that includes multiple centuries and continents. The inevitability of distinction and exclusion is not at odds with the unity of the church and her orthodoxy. On the contrary, not only do creeds and confessions signal distinction and exclusion, but they communicate the nature of the church. Members of Christ's church are in corporate solidarity and unity with the saints of old who were baptized in the name of the triune God, confessed Jesus as Savior and Lord, and received the Spirit who gives us life in the Son.

This means that diverse traditions can also enjoy a substantial unity. While the particulars of any of our denominations or our theological heritage give us distinction from one another, the

---

[2] Fesko, *The Need for Creeds Today*, xvi.

universal substance of our shared inheritance gives unity. While we may disagree on particulars of doctrine, such as baptism or the Lord's Supper, we have meaningful unity in the realm of theology proper, trinitarianism, Christology, soteriology, and the like.

To Be Used in the Church's Liturgy

What a wondrous thought that on any given Lord's Day, millions of Christians around the world are confessing belief in and love for the triune God who has transferred them from the kingdom of darkness to the kingdom of God's beloved Son, in whom they have redemption, the forgiveness of sins. Incorporating a historical creed in the weekly Lord's Day service can serve as a tangible reminder to all present in a local assembly of this vital truth.

How churches might incorporate creedal use in the liturgical life can vary in a number of ways. When a church confesses a creed together—perhaps in the call to worship, or *before* the preaching ministry takes place—they remind the congregation, *this* is the God we are about to hear from in the proclamation of Scripture. Other congregations might find the Lord's Supper to be an appropriate place, since communion is a meal for the saints and since historical creeds can remind us what a true Christian profession of the faith sounds like. Or perhaps some congregations see the benediction on any given Lord's Day as the proper place to recite the creed because it reminds the church that we leave here united with each other member *and* with the saints of yesterday under *this* same faith.

The authors of this book have seen creeds (and confessions) used in each of these sections of a church's liturgical rhythm in ways that honored the Lord, united the saints, and guarded the church's witness. Bringing creeds and confessions into your particular ecclesial context may come with challenges and obstacles. However, the payoff of proper unity, proper doctrine, and a proper confession in the regular gathering of the church is worth the work it takes to establish the creeds in the everyday life of the church.

In what follows we have included four creeds from the church catholic (universal) that have had considerable impact and carry no little authority. Two of these are from ecumenical councils—the Nicene Creed and the Chalcedonian Definition of Christology. The other two are creeds regarded with much esteem through the history of the church—the Apostles' Creed and the Athanasian Creed—recited in the liturgy of churches each Sunday.[3]

---

[3] These four creeds are taken from Chad Van Dixhoorn, *Creeds, Confessions, and Catechisms: A Readers Edition* (Wheaton, IL: Crossway, 2022), hereinafter, Van Dixhoorn, *Creeds*.

The Apostles' Creed

I believe in God the Father Almighty,
    Maker of heaven and earth.

I believe in Jesus Christ, his only-begotten Son, our Lord;
    who was conceived by the Holy Spirit, born of the Virgin Mary;
    suffered under Pontius Pilate;
    was crucified, dead, and buried;
    he descended into hell;
    the third day he rose again from the dead;
    he ascended into heaven,
    and sits at the right hand of God the Father Almighty;
    from there he shall come to judge the living and the dead.

I believe in the Holy Spirit;
    the holy catholic church;
    the communion of saints;
    the forgiveness of sins;
    the resurrection of the body;
    and the life everlasting. Amen.

The Nicene Creed

I believe in one God, the Father Almighty,
    Maker of heaven and earth, and
    of all things visible and invisible.

And in one Lord Jesus Christ, the only-begotten Son of God,
    begotten of the Father before all worlds;

God of God, Light of Light,
very God of very God;
begotten, not made,
being of the one substance with the Father,
by whom all things were made.
Who, for us men and for our salvation,
came down from heaven
and was incarnate by the Holy Spirit of the Virgin Mary,
and was made man;
and was crucified also for us under Pontius Pilate;
he suffered and was buried;
and the third day he rose again, according to the Scriptures;
and ascended into heaven,
and sits on the right hand of the Father;
and he shall come again, with glory,
to judge the living and the dead;
whose kingdom shall have no end.

And I believe in the Holy Spirit,
    the Lord and Giver of life;
    who proceeds from the Father and the Son;
    who with the Father and the Son together is worshiped and glorified;
    who spoke by the prophets.
    And I believe in one holy catholic and apostolic church.
    I acknowledge one baptism for the remission of sins;
    and I look for the resurrection of the dead,
    and the life of the world to come. Amen.

The Chalcedonian Definition

Following the saintly fathers, we all with one voice teach the confession of one and the same Son, our Lord Jesus Christ: the same perfect in divinity and perfect in humanity, the same truly God and truly man, of a rational soul and a body; consubstantial with the Father as regards his divinity, and the same consubstantial with us as regards his humanity; like us in all respects except for sin; begotten before the ages from the Father as regards his divinity, and in the last days the same for us and for our salvation from Mary, the virgin God-bearer, as regards his humanity; one and the same Christ, Son, Lord, only-begotten, acknowledged in two natures which undergo no confusion, no change, no division, no separation; at no point was the difference between the natures taken away through the union, but rather the property of both natures is preserved and comes together into a single person and a single subsistent being; he is not parted or divided into two persons, but is one and the same only-begotten Son, God, Word, Lord Jesus Christ, just as the prophets taught from the beginning about him, and as the Lord Jesus Christ himself instructed us, and as the creed of the fathers handed it down to us.

The Athanasian Creed

Whoever desires to be saved should above all hold to the catholic faith. Anyone who does not keep it whole and unbroken will doubtless perish eternally.

Now this is the catholic faith: that we worship one God in Trinity and the Trinity in unity, neither confounding their persons nor dividing the essence. For the person of the Father is a distinct person, the person of the Son is another, and that of the Holy Spirit still another. But the divinity of the Father, Son, and Holy Spirit is one, the glory equal, the majesty coeternal. Such as the Father is, such is the Son and such is the Holy Spirit. The Father is uncreated, the Son is uncreated, the Holy Spirit is uncreated. The Father is immeasurable, the Son is immeasurable, the Holy Spirit is immeasurable. The Father is eternal, the Son is eternal, the Holy Spirit is eternal. And yet there are not three eternal beings; there is but one eternal being. So too there are not three uncreated or immeasurable beings; there is but one uncreated and immeasurable being. Similarly, the Father is almighty, the Son is almighty, the Holy Spirit is almighty. Yet there are not three almighty beings; there is but one almighty being. Thus, the Father is God, the Son is God, the Holy Spirit is God. Yet there are not three gods; there is but one God. Thus, the Father is Lord, the Son is Lord, the Holy Spirit is Lord. Yet there are not three lords; there is but one Lord. Just as Christian truth compels us to confess each person individually as both God and Lord, so catholic religion forbids us to say that there are three gods or lords. The Father was neither made nor created nor begotten from anyone. The Son was neither made nor created; he was begotten from the Father alone. The Holy Spirit was neither made nor created nor begotten; he proceeds from the Father and the Son. Accordingly, there is one Father, not three fathers; there is one Son, not three sons; there is one Holy Spirit, not three holy spirits. None in this Trinity is before or after, none is greater or smaller; in their entirety the three persons are coeternal and coequal with each other. So in everything, as was said earlier, the unity in Trinity, and the Trinity in unity, is to be worshiped. Anyone then who desires to be saved should think thus about the Trinity.

But it is necessary for eternal salvation that one also believe in the incarnation of our Lord Jesus Christ faithfully. Now this is the true faith: that we believe and confess that our Lord Jesus Christ,

God's Son, is both God and man, equally. He is God from the essence of the Father, begotten before time; and he is man from the essence of his mother, born in time; completely God, completely man, with a rational soul and human flesh; equal to the Father as regards divinity, less than the Father as regards humanity. Although he is God and man, yet Christ is not two, but one. He is one, however, not by his divinity being turned into flesh, but by God's taking humanity to himself. He is one, certainly not by the blending of his essence, but by the unity of his person. For just as one man is both rational soul and flesh, so too the one Christ is both God and man. He suffered for our salvation; he descended to hell; he arose from the dead on the third day; he ascended to heaven; he is seated at the Father's right hand; from there he will come to judge the living and the dead. At his coming all people will arise bodily and give an accounting of their own deeds. Those who have done good will enter eternal life, and those who have done evil will enter eternal fire.

This is the catholic faith: that one cannot be saved without believing it firmly and faithfully.

SELECTED BIBLIOGRAPHY

Primary Sources

Alighieri, Dante. *The Divine Comedy: The Inferno, The Purgatorio, The Paradiso.* Translated by John Ciardi. New York: New American Library, 2003.

Anselm. *The Major Works: Monologion, Proslogion, and Why God Became Man.* Oxford: Oxford University Press, 1998.

Aquinas, Thomas. *Commentary on the Gospel of John: Chapters 1–5.* Translated by Fabian Larcher and James A. Weisheipl. Washington, DC: Catholic University of America Press, 2010.

———. *Commentary on the Gospel of John: Chapters 13–21.* Translated by Fabian Larcher and James A. Weisheipl. Washington, DC: Catholic University of America Press, 2010.

———. *Summa Theologiae.* Vol. 2, *Existence and Nature of God, 1a, 2–11.* Cambridge: Cambridge University Press, 2006.

———. *Summa Theologiae.* Vol. 6, *The Trinity, 1a, 27–32.* Cambridge: Cambridge University Press, 2006.

———. *Summa Theologiae.* Vol. 7, *Father, Son, and Holy Ghost, 1a, 33–43.* Cambridge: Cambridge University Press, 2006.

———. *Summa Theologiae.* Vol 48, *The Incarnate Word, 3a, 1–6.* Cambridge: Cambridge University Press, 2006.

Athanasius. *Against the Arians*. In vol. 4 of *Nicene and Post-Nicene Fathers*, Series 1. Edited by Philip Schaff. Peabody, MA: Hendrickson, 1999.

———. *De Decretis*. In vol. 4 of *Nicene and Post-Nicene Fathers*, Series 2. Edited by Philip Schaff. Peabody, MA: Hendrickson, 1999.

Augustine. *Confessions*. Oxford: Oxford University Press, 1991.

———. *De Trinitate*. Edited by John E. Rotelle OSA and Edmund Hill OP. 2nd ed. Hyde Park, NY: New City Press, 2012.

———. *The Works of Augustine,* Part 2. Translated by Roland J. Teske. Hyde Park, NY: New City Press, 2003.

Basil of Caesarea. *On the Holy Spirit*. Crestwood, NY: St. Vladimir's Press, 2011.

Bavinck, Herman. *Reformed Dogmatics*. Vol. 2, *God and Creation*. Edited by John Bolt. Translated by John Vriend. Grand Rapids: Baker Academic, 2004.

Boethius. *Theological Tractates*. LCL. Translated by H. F. Stewart, E. K. Rand, and A. J. Tester. Cambridge, MA: Harvard University Press, 1973.

Brakel, Wilhelmus à. *The Christian's Reasonable Service*. 4 vols. Translated by Bartel Elshout. Edited by Joel R. Beeke. Grand Rapids: Reformation Heritage Books, 1992.

Calvin, John. *Calvin's Commentaries: XVII: John*. Grand Rapids: Baker, 2009.

———. *Institutes of the Christian Religion*. Vol. 1. Edited by John T. McNeill. Translated by Ford Lewis Battles. Louisville: Westminster John Knox, 1960.

Charnock, Stephen. *The Existence and Attributes of God*. 1853. Reprint, Grand Rapids, MI: Baker, 1979.

Cyril of Alexandria. *On the Unity of Christ*. Popular Patristics Series, vol. 13. Crestwood, NY: St. Vladimir's Seminary Press, 1995.

Gill, John. *A Complete Body of Doctrinal and Practical Divinity*. Paris, AR: The Baptist Standard Bearer, 2007.

Gregory of Nazianzus. *On God and Christ*. Crestwood, NY: St Vladimir's Seminary Press, 2002.

Gregory of Nyssa. *Against Eunomius*. In *Nicene and Post-Nicene Fathers*, Series 2. Edited by Philip Schaff and Henry Wace. Vol. 5. Peabody, MA: Hendrickson, 2012.

———. *On the Holy Trinity*. Vol. 5 in *Nicene and Post-Nicene Fathers*, Series 2. Edited by Philip Schaff. Peabody, MA: Hendrickson, 1999.

Hilary of Poitiers. *De Trinitate*. In vol. 9 of *Nicene and Post-Nicene Fathers*, Series 2. Edited by Philip Schaff, W. Sunday, and Henry Wace. Translated by E. W. Watson and L. Pullan. Peabody, MA: Hendrickson, 1999.

Irenaeus. *Against Heresies*. In vol. 1 of *The Faith of the Early Fathers*. Translated by William Jurgens. Collegeville: The Liturgical Press, 1970.

John of Damascus. *Exposition of the Orthodox Faith*. Vol. 9 in *Nicene and Post-Nicene Fathers*, Series 2. Edited by Philip Schaff, W. Sunday, and Henry Wace. Translated by E. W. Watson and L. Pullan. Peabody, MA: Hendrickson, 1999.

———. *The Fathers of the Church: John of Damascus: Writings*, vol. 37. Translated by Frederic H. Chase Jr. Washington, DC: Catholic University of America Press, 1999.

Junius, Franciscus. *Synopsis Purioris Theologiae / Synopsis of a Purer Theology: Latin Text and English Translation*. Vol. 1, *Disputations 1–23*, edited by H. van der Belt, et al. Studies in Medieval and Reformation Tradition 187. Leiden: Brill, 2014.

———. *A Treatise on True Theology: With the Life of Franciscus Junius*. Translated by David C. Noe. Grand Rapids: Reformation Heritage Books, 2014.

Leigh, Edward. *A Systeme or Body of Divinity.* London: A.M., 1662.

Luther, Martin. *The Three Symbols or Creeds of the Christian Faith,* in *Luther's Works.* Philadelphia, PA: Fortress Press, 1960.

Mastricht, Petrus van. *Theoretical-Practical Theology.* Vol. 2, *Faith in the Triune God,* edited by Joel R. Beeke. Grand Rapids: Reformation Heritage Books, 2019.

Maximus the Confessor. *The Cosmic Mystery of Christ.* Crestwood, NY: St Vladimir's Seminary Press, 2003.

Owen, John. *Brief Vindication.* In *The Works of John Owen,* vol. 2, edited by William Goold. Reprint, Edinburgh: Banner of Truth Trust, 2009.

———. *Vindicae Evangelicae.* In *The Works of John Owen,* vol. 12, edited by William Goold. Reprint, Edinburgh: Banner of Truth Trust, 2009.

Pictet, Benedict. *Christian Theology.* Translated by Frederick Reyroux. London: Seeley and Sons, 1834.

Turretin, Francis. *Institutes of Elenctic Theology.* Vol. 1. Phillipsburg: P&R, 1992.

Secondary Sources

Allen, Michael, ed. *Theological Commentary: Evangelical Perspectives.* London: T&T Clark, 2011.

——— and Scott R. Swain. *Reformed Catholicity: The Promise of Retrieval for Theology and Biblical Interpretation.* Grand Rapids: Baker Academic, 2015.

——— and Scott R. Swain, eds. *Christian Dogmatics: Reformed Theology for the Church Catholic.* Grand Rapids: Eerdmans, 2016.

———. *Grounded in Heaven: Recentering Christian Hope and Life on God.* Grand Rapids: Baker Academic, 2018.

Anatolios, Khaled. *Retrieving Nicaea: The Development and Meaning of Trinitarian Doctrine.* Grand Rapids: Baker Academic, 2018.

Ayres, Lewis. *Nicaea and Its Legacy: An Approach to Fourth-Century Trinitarian Theology.* Oxford: Oxford University Press, 2009.

Barrett, Matthew. *None Greater: The Undomesticated Attributes of God.* Grand Rapids: Baker, 2019.

———. *The Reformation as Renewal: Retrieving the One, Holy, Catholic, and Apostolic Church.* Grand Rapids: Zondervan Academic, 2023.

———. *Simply Trinity: The Unmanipulated Father, Son, and Spirit.* Grand Rapids: Baker, 2021.

———, ed. *On Classical Trinitarianism: Retrieving the Nicene Doctrine of the Triune God.* Downers Grove, IL: IVP Academic, 2025.

Bates, Matthew W. *The Birth of the Trinity: Jesus, God, and Spirit in New Testament and Early Christian Interpretations of the Old Testament.* Oxford: Oxford University Press, 2016.

Behr, John. *The Way to Nicaea.* 3 vols. New York: St Vladimir's Press, 2001.

Bird, Michael F., and Scott Harrower, eds. *Trinity Without Hierarchy: Reclaiming Nicene Orthodoxy in Evangelical Theology.* Grand Rapids: Kregel Academic, 2019.

Butner, D. Glenn, Jr. *The Son Who Learned Obedience: A Theological Case Against the Eternal Submission of the Son.* Eugene: Pickwick, 2018.

———. *Trinitarian Dogmatics: Exploring the Grammar of the Christian Doctrine of God.* Grand Rapids: Baker Academic, 2022.

Carson, D. A. *The Gospel According to John.* PNTC. Grand Rapids: Eerdmans, 1990.

Carter, Craig A. *Contemplating God with the Great Tradition: Recovering Trinitarian Classical Theism*. Grand Rapids: Baker Academic, 2021.

———. *Interpreting Scripture with the Great Tradition: Recovering the Genius of Premodern Exegesis*. Grand Rapids: Baker Academic, 2018.

Cary, Phillip. *The Nicene Creed: An Introduction*. Bellingham, WA: Lexham, 2023.

Chesterton, G. K. *The Everlasting Man*. Moscow, ID: Canon Press, 2021.

Dale, Robert William. *Christian Doctrine*. London: Hodder & Stoughton, 1894.

Dolezal, James E. *All That Is in God: Evangelical Theology and the Challenge of Classical Christian Theism*. Grand Rapids: Reformation Heritage Books, 2017.

———. *God without Parts: Divine Simplicity and the Metaphysics of God's Absoluteness*. Eugene: Pickwick Publications, 2011.

———. "Trinity, Simplicity and the Status of God's Personal Relations." *International Journal of Systematic Theology* 16, no. 1 (2014): 79–98.

Duby, Steven J. *Divine Simplicity: A Dogmatic Account*. London: T&T Clark, 2016.

———. *God in Himself: Scripture, Metaphysics, and the Task of Christian Theology*. Downers Grove, IL: IVP Academic, 2019.

———. *Jesus and the God of Classical Theism: Biblical Christology in Light of the Doctrine of God*. Grand Rapids: Baker Academic, 2022.

Emery, Gilles. *The Trinitarian Theology of St Thomas Aquinas*. Oxford: Oxford University Press, 2010.

---. *The Trinity: An Introduction to Catholic Doctrine on the Triune God*. Translated by Matthew Levering. Washington, DC: Catholic University of America Press, 2011.

--- and Matthew Levering, eds. *The Oxford Handbook on the Trinity*. Oxford: Oxford University Press, 2014.

Fesko, J. V. *The Need for Creeds Today: Confessional Faith in a Faithless Age*. Grand Rapids: Baker Academic, 2020.

---. *The Trinity and the Covenant of Redemption*. Fern, UK: Mentor, 2016.

Giles, Kevin. *The Eternal Generation of the Son: Maintaining Orthodoxy in Trinitarian Theology*. Downers Grove, IL: IVP Academic, 2012.

Grillmeier, Aloys. *Christ in Christian Tradition*. Vol. 1, *From the Apostolic Age to Chalcedon (451)*. Translated by John Bowden. Atlanta: John Knox Press, 1975.

Grudem, Wayne. *Systematic Theology*. 2nd ed. Grand Rapids: Zondervan Academic, 2022.

Hanson, R. P. C. *The Search for the Christian God: The Arian Controversy*. Grand Rapids: Baker Academic, 2005.

Holmes, Christopher R. J. *The Holy Spirit*. New Studies in Dogmatics. Grand Rapids: Zondervan, 2015.

Jacobson, Rolf A., and Beth LaNeel Tanner. "Book One of the Psalter: Psalms 1–41." In *The Book of Psalms*, edited by Nancy deClaissé-Walford, Rolf A. Jacobson, and Beth LaNeel Tanner, 55–384. Grand Rapids: Eerdmans, 2014.

Jamieson, R. B., and Tyler R. Wittman. *Biblical Reasoning: Christological and Trinitarian Rules for Exegesis*. Grand Rapids: Baker Academic, 2022.

Kidner, Derek. *Psalms 1–72: An Introduction and Commentary*. Downers Grove, IL: IVP, 1973.

Köstenberger, Andreas. *Encountering John*. Encountering Biblical Studies. Grand Rapids: Baker, 2013.

Kurtz, Ronni. *No Shadow of Turning: Divine Immutability and the Economy of Redemption*. Fearn, UK: Christian Mentor, 2022.

Legge, Dominic. *The Trinitarian Christology of St. Thomas Aquinas*. Oxford: Oxford University Press, 2017.

Lewis, C. S. *The Chronicles of Narnia: The Last Battle*. New York: HarperCollins, 1984.

———. *God in the Dock: Essays on Theology and Ethics*. Edited by Walter Hooper. Grand Rapids: Eerdmans, 1970.

———. *Surprised by Joy: The Shape of My Early Life*. New York: Harcourt Brace, 1955.

McGuckin, John Anthony. *The Path of Christianity: The First Thousand Years*. Grand Rapids: IVP Academic, 2017.

McGraw, Ryan M. *By Good and Necessary Consequence*. Explorations in Reformed Confessional Theology. Grand Rapids, MI: Reformation Heritage Books, 2012.

Moreland, J. P., and William Lane Craig. *Philosophical Foundations for a Christian Worldview*. 2nd ed. Downers Grove, IL: IVP Academic, 2017.

Muller, Richard A. *Dictionary of Latin and Greek Theological Terms: Drawn Principally from Protestant Scholastic Theology*. 2nd ed. Grand Rapids: Baker Academic, 2017.

———. *Post-Reformation Reformed Dogmatics*. Vol. 4, *The Triunity of God*. Grand Rapids: Baker Academic, 2003.

Needham, Nick, ed. *Daily Readings: The Early Church Fathers*. Fearn, UK: Christian Focus, 2017.

Ortlund, Gavin. *Theological Retrieval for Evangelicals: Why We Need Our Past to Have a Future*. Wheaton, IL: Crossway, 2019.

Parkison, Samuel G. *To Gaze Upon God: The Beatific Vision in Doctrine, Tradition, and Practice*. Downers Grove, IL: IVP Academic, 2024.

Pelikan, Jaroslav, and Valerie Hotchkiss R. *Creeds & Confessions of Faith in the Christian Tradition*. New Haven: Yale University Press, 2003.

Pierce, Madison N. *Divine Discourse in the Epistle to the Hebrews: The Recontextualization of Spoken Quotations in Scripture*. Cambridge: Cambridge University Press, 2020.

Plumer, William S. *Psalms: A Critical and Expository Commentary with Doctrinal and Practical Remarks*. 1975. Reprinted, Edinburgh: Banner of Truth Trust, 1978.

Rahner, Karl. *The Trinity*. New York: Crossroad, 1997.

Renihan, James M. *To the Judicious and Impartial Reader*. Baptist Symbolics 2, *A Contextual-Historical Exposition of the Second London Baptist Confession of Faith*. Cape Coral, FL: Founders Press, 2022.

Rusch, William G., ed. *The Trinitarian Controversy*. Philadelphia: Fortress Press, 1980.

Sanders, Fred. *The Triune God*. New Studies in Dogmatics. Grand Rapids: Zondervan, 2016.

———. and Scott R. Swain, eds. *Retrieving Eternal Generation*. Grand Rapids: Zondervan, 2017.

Saner, Andrea D. *Too Much to Grasp: Exodus 3:13–15 and the Reality of God*. University Park: Eisenbrauns, 2015.

Smith, Brandon D. *The Biblical Trinity: Encountering the Father, Son, and Holy Spirit in Scripture*. Bellingham, WA: Lexham, 2023.

———. *The Trinity in the Book of Revelation: Seeing Father, Son, and Holy Spirit in John's Apocalypse*. Downers Grove, IL: IVP Academic, 2022.

Spurgeon, Charles Haddon, "The Immutability of God—Mal. 3:6." In *New Park Street Pulpit*. Vol. 1. 1855. Public domain.

Swain, Scott R. *The Trinity and the Bible: On Theological Interpretation*. Bellingham, WA: Lexham Press, 2021.

———. *The Trinity: An Introduction*. Wheaton, IL: Crossway, 2021.

Tabb, Brian J., and Andrew M. King, eds. *Five Views of Christ in the Old Testament*. Grand Rapids: Zondervan Academic, 2022.

Trueman, Carl R. *The Creedal Imperative*. Wheaton, IL: Crossway, 2012.

Van Dixhoorn, Chad. *Creeds, Confessions, and Catechisms: A Reader's Edition*. Wheaton, IL: Crossway, 2022.

Vidu, Adonis. *Divine Missions: An Introduction*. Eugene, OR: Cascade Books, 2021.

———. *The Same God Who Works All Things: Inseparable Operations in Trinitarian Theology*. Grand Rapids: Eerdmans, 2021.

Ware, Bruce A. *Father, Son, and Spirit: Relationships, Roles, and Relevance*. Wheaton, IL: Crossway, 2005.

Warfield, Benjamin Breckinridge. "The Biblical Doctrine of the Trinity." In *Biblical Doctrines*. Vol. 2 of *The Works of Benjamin B. Warfield*. Reprint, Grand Rapids: Baker, 2003.

Webster, John. *God Without Measure: Working Papers in Christian Theology*. Vol. 1, *God and the Works of God*. London: T&T Clark, 2018.

Weinandy, Thomas Gerard. *Does God Change? The Word's Becoming in the Incarnation*. Still River, MA: St. Bede's Publications, 1985.

———. *Does God Suffer?* Notre Dame: University of Notre Dame Press, 2000.

White, Thomas Joseph. *The Incarnate Lord: A Thomistic Study in Christology.* Washington, DC: The Catholic University of America Press, 2017.

———. *The Trinity: On the Nature and Mystery of the One God.* Washington, DC: The Catholic University of America Press, 2022.

Whitfield, Keith S., ed. *Trinitarian Theology: Theological Models and Doctrinal Applications.* Nashville: B&H Academic, 2019.

Wuellner, Bernard. *Dictionary of Scholastic Philosophy.* Fitzwilliam, NH: Loreto, 2012.

SUBJECT INDEX

A
Aaron (high priest), 22
Aaronic Benediction, 61–62
Abihu (son of Aaron), 22–23
Abraham (father of Israel), 60, 104–5
ad extra, 57, 91, 96, 153, 160, 167. See also Trinity: ontological
ad intra, 57, 91, 93, 95, 159–60, 164. See also Trinity: economy of
adoption (by God), 59, 63, 67, 169
Adoptionism, 115
Alexander (bishop of Alexandria), 31–32
Alighieri, Dante, 138
Ambrose, 155
Anabaptists, 5
analogical language, 135
Anselm of Canterbury, 94, 171
anti-Nicene figures, 34
Apostles' Creed, 189–90
apostles, 50, 139

Aquinas, Thomas, 58–59, 76, 82, 88, 94, 161–65, 171
Arianism, 24, 31, 34, 84–86, 115
Arians, 33, 84–88, 94, 111, 127, 155
Arius, 30–32, 35–36, 84, 109, 126
Asaph (psalmist), 52
ascension, the, 13–14, 48, 98, 132, 140, 167, 169, 184, 190–91, 194
aseity, 35, 65, 76. See also Trinity: self-sufficiency of
Athanasian Creed, 71–77, 95, 163, 189, 192–94
Athanasius, 31–35, 58, 71–72, 88, 94, 155
atonement, 98, 126, 139, 151, 169
attributes of God, 13, 37, 65, 76–77, 110, 136, 159
Augustine, 52, 94, 96, 105, 153, 155, 162, 171, 179

B

baptism
    of believers, 19, 26, 50, 56, 67, 139–40, 169, 184, 187, 191
    doctrine of, 188
    of Jesus, 53, 59, 66
Barrett, Matthew, 2–3, 5, 88, 101, 116
Basil of Caesarea, 56, 68, 127–29, 149, 157
Basil the Great, 133. *See* Basil of Caesarea
Bavinck, Herman, 69
beatific vision, 43, 140, 152, 170–77, 182
Biblical Trinity, The (Smith), 3
biblicism
    naïve, 5
body of Christ, 140–41
Butner, D. Glenn, Jr., 40, 104
Byzantium (empire), 141–42

C

Calvin, John, 57, 65, 171
Cappadocian Fathers, 94, 127, 131
Carson, D. A., 51, 64, 106
Carter, Craig A., 6
catechesis, 26, 169
catholicism, 4, 73–74, 192–94
Catholicism, Roman, 142
centers of consciousness, 90–93, 153. *See also* Trinity: will of
Cerularius, Michael, 142
Chalcedonian Creed, 122
Chalcedonian Definition, 166, 189, 192. *See* Chalcedonian Creed
Charnock, Stephen, 8
Chesterton, G. K., 4–5
Christendom, 141
Christology, 34, 105, 113–14, 186–88
church
    apostolic, 139–40, 184, 191
    catholic, 8, 72, 100, 139–40, 184, 189–91
    challenges faced today by, 89–95
    contemporary, 100, 182, 186
    in Corinth, 73, 182
    early, 99, 126, 155, 159, 181
    Eastern, 141–42. *See also* Eastern Orthodox Church
    in Ephesus, 121
    evangelical, 93
    history of, 26, 40, 55, 71, 83–84, 99, 110, 149, 183, 185
    in Jerusalem, 107
    Jesus as head of, 97
    life of, 71, 102, 115, 185–94. *See* "Appendix," (185–94)
    local, 30, 113, 138
    reading Scripture with, 8, 20, 49
    Western, 72, 141–42
    worship in, 30, 72, 186, 188
church fathers, 18, 51, 71, 133, 149, 179
communion of saints, 187, 190

communion (sacrament), 188. *See also* Eucharist; Lord's Table
confession (of belief), 7, 17, 19, 24, 38, 40, 44, 73, 81, 112, 114–15, 119, 134, 181–82, 185–89, 192–93
confessions, Christian, 1, 5–6, 53, 111, 117, 182–83, 185, 187–88. *See also* creeds, Christian
Constantine, 32
Constantinopolitan Creed, 32. *See also* Nicene Creed; Nicene-Constantinopolitan Creed
consubstantiation, 40, 110, 112, 122, 129, 192
Contemplating God with the Great Tradition (Carter), 6
contemplation (spiritual discipline), 6, 28–29, 46–47, 51, 57, 60, 62, 69–71, 96–98, 111, 125, 134, 171, 173, 180, 182
Council of Constantinople, 126
Council of Nicaea, 31–32, 84, 99–100
Council of Toledo, 141–42
creatio ex nihilo, 53, 85
creeds, Christian, 1, 5–8, 72, 111–12, 114–15, 138, 185–94. *See appendix* (185–89); *see also* confessions, Christian
cross, the, 11–13, 131–32, 139, 148, 151, 154, 166
crucifixion, 12, 85, 95, 184, 190–91

D

Dante, 138
David (king), 10–13, 29, 171–75
divine appropriations, 63, 152, 161–69
Divine Comedy, The (Dante), 138
divine decree, the, 159–61
divine simplicity, 1, 12, 35, 71–96, 102, 117, 135, 159. *See chapter 3, "One God in Trinity"* (71–96)
divine singularity, 37, 152, 155, 159, 161
dogmatics, 69
Dolezal, James, 82–83, 89
double procession, 122, 138
doxology, 3, 8, 30, 36, 50, 66–68, 71, 152

E

Eastern Orthodox Church, 142. *See also* church: Eastern
economy of salvation, 34, 96, 98, 118, 135, 144, 163
Edwards, Jonathan, 28
Emery, Gilles, 56, 163, 165
Emmaus Church (North Kansas City, MO), 2
equivocal language, 135
essence, divine, 76–77, 84, 89, 168, 176. *See also homoousios*; nature, divine; substance, divine

of Father, 83–85, 87, 94–95, 109, 156, 194
indivisibility of, 37–38, 72, 74, 82–83, 96, 101–2, 112, 152, 192
oneness of, 14, 33, 37–38, 40, 72, 79, 82, 90, 101–2, 109, 112, 120, 136, 153, 162, 164
"of the same essence," 31
simplicity of, 82, 90, 93, 102, 112, 157–58, 164
of Son, 83, 87, 94, 110, 122
of Trinity, 31–32, 35, 57, 74, 83, 88, 90, 92–93, 102, 109, 112, 114–15, 136, 153, 156, 161
eternal functional subordination of the Son (EFS), 92–95, 112, 115, 117
eternal generation of the Son, 1, 34, 39, 57–59, 80–81, 83, 88–89, 91–92, 94, 97–123, 127, 136, 139, 143, 183. *See chapter 4, "The Son and His Father," (97–123)*
eternal processions, 8, 57, 103, 106, 143, 165
evangelicals, 7, 24, 30, 91–92, 170
evangelism, 19
exegesis, 7, 13, 32, 63, 104, 106
  modern, 171
  prosopological, 62
  second, 6
Exposition of the Orthodox Faith, An (John of Damascus), 110

F

faith, 1, 7, 13, 18–20, 24, 26, 30, 49, 51–52, 56, 60, 69, 74, 110, 140–41, 150, 170, 174, 180–83, 185–88, 192–94
Father
  as begetter, 38–39, 79, 81, 85, 87–88, 112, 120, 138, 156, 158
  communion of believers with, 57, 65, 70, 168
  innascibility, 80, 82
  person of, 53, 81, 99, 102, 106, 114, 192
  as principle (source) of Son, 79–80, 82, 102, 114
  unbegottenness of, 59, 79, 82, 102, 110, 112, 114, 118, 138, 156, 158, 169, 183, 193
filiation, 80, 82–83, 88–89, 107, 114, 143. *See also* Son: begottenness of
filioque, 141–45
First Cause, 76

G

Gill, John, 116, 181
glory (divine attribute), 9–11, 13–14, 28, 35, 40, 42–43, 45–46, 56, 64–65, 68–69, 78–79, 85, 92, 95, 101, 111, 115, 120, 125, 127, 133–34, 136, 140, 174, 182, 184–85, 191, 193

Godhead, 46, 79–81, 95–96, 105, 109, 113, 115, 144, 153, 156
gospel (message), 44, 48, 60, 139
Great Schism, 142
Gregory of Nazianzus, 78, 127, 129–30, 155
Gregory of Nyssa, 18, 96, 116, 127, 155, 157, 171

H

Herbert, George, 41–43
Hilary of Poitiers, 155
history of salvation, 57–58, 60, 66, 163
holiness (divine attribute), 37, 56, 76, 121–23, 125, 144, 160, 163
Holy Spirit. *See* Spirit
homoiousios, 99
homoousios, 31, 58, 99, 102, 110, 114, 156. *See also* essence, divine; nature, divine; substance, divine
humility, 26–27, 49, 51, 58, 68
hypostatic union, 165–66

I

idolatry, 20, 22, 73, 78
immutability (divine attribute), 63–64, 84–85, 89, 98
impassibility (divine attribute), 84–85
incarnation, the, 12–14, 59, 117, 144, 161, 164, 183, 191
incomprehensibility of God, 8, 19, 41, 47, 50, 58, 84, 111, 131, 135, 138
inseparable operations, 1, 8, 13–14, 63, 119, 151–77. *See chapter 6, "Communion with the Undivided Trinity,"* (151–77)
intra-trinitarian taxis, 144
Isaiah (prophet), 171
Israel (nation), 11, 22, 37–38, 64, 73, 78

J

Jacobson, Rolf, 172
Jamieson, R. B., 8, 159
Jeremiah (prophet), 23
Jesus Christ, 50. *See also* Son; Word, divine
 as Davidic King, 12–13
 death of, 12–13, 95, 98, 122, 131, 139, 166, 169, 190
 as God-man, 13, 165
 life of, 98, 139, 169
 miracles of, 86, 166
 oneness with Father, 34
 as Second Adam, 140
 union of believers with, 98, 140, 143–44, 169
Job (biblical figure), 171
John (apostle), 10, 40, 64, 87, 145, 171
John of Damascus, 58–59, 109–12, 163
Judaism, 78
Jude (brother of Jesus), 149

K

Kent, John, 144
Kidner, Derek, 173

L

Leo IX (pope), 142
Lewis, C. S., 27, 29, 41, 119, 150
Ligonier Ministries, 23
    State of Theology report, 23, 2020
liturgy, 50, 71–72, 186, 188–89. *See also* worship
Logos, divine, 34
Lord's Supper, 188
Lord's Table, 140. *See also* communion (sacrament)
love (divine attribute), 37, 44, 48, 51, 76, 125, 132, 139, 145, 150, 155, 169–70
Luther, Martin, 72

M

Macedonius, 126–27
Mary (mother of Jesus), 106, 122, 140, 183, 190–92
Mastricht, Petrus van, 105, 159, 161
Maximus the Confessor, 166
modalism, 14, 82, 156
monogenēs, 104
monotheism, 38, 48, 73, 78–79, 99, 154
Moses (prophet), 22, 63–64, 73, 170–71, 173

N

Nadab (son of Aaron), 22–23
nature, divine. *See also homoousios*; essence, divine; substance, divine
    of Father, 88, 123
    oneness of, 33, 37–38, 40, 156
    shared by Father and Son, 39, 88
    simplicity of, 37, 156
    of Son, 12, 84–86, 122, 165, 186
    of Spirit, 140
    of Trinity, 33, 82, 90, 127, 136, 138, 168
    triunity of, 8, 19, 27, 43–44, 62, 69
New Testament use of Old Testament, 66
Nicene-Constantinopolitan Creed, 32, 141. *See also* Constantinopolitan Creed; Nicene Creed
Nicene Creed, 32, 36–40, 53, 71, 89, 92, 94, 108–11, 114, 122, 134, 139, 163–64, 189–91. *See also* Constantinopolitan Creed; Nicene-Constantinopolitan Creed

O

oikonomia, 34, 57, 159–60. *See also* Trinity: economy of

omnipotence (divine attribute), 110, 155
omnipresence (divine attribute), 110, 132
omniscience (divine attribute), 53
On the Holy Spirit (Basil), 127, 157
"Oration 31" (Gregory of Nazianzus), 129
orthodoxy, 5, 24, 35–36, 83–89, 95, 100, 115
Owen, John, 70, 77, 82, 90, 94, 167–69, 171

P

papacy, 142
Paradiso (Dante), 138
passive potency, 75, 88
paternity (divine), 79, 82, 107, 114, 143
paterology, 99, 102
Paul (apostle), 25, 38, 41, 45, 60, 66, 69, 73–75, 121, 127, 134, 137, 146, 150, 155, 171, 180, 182, 186
Pentecost, 50, 59, 61, 66, 68, 107, 133, 140, 164–65
personal appropriations, 157
Peter (apostle), 18, 98, 107, 142
Pharisees, 104–5
Plumer, William S., 174–75
Pneumatomachi, 127, 129
power (divine attribute), 10, 22, 33, 35, 59, 68, 76, 79, 86, 97, 100, 111, 120, 125, 133, 136, 155–56, 159–60, 162–63
prayer, 6, 19, 45, 49, 127, 129, 151–52, 168–69, 171
  of David, 171–75
  of Jesus Christ, 148
  of Paul, 25, 69
  the Spirit and, 145–48, 150
prodigal son, 116
pro-Nicene fathers, 33–34, 155
propitiation, 48, 123
protective application, 113–17
provisional application, 113, 117–23
pure act, 77, 88–89

R

Radicals (opposite the Reformers), 5
Rahner, Karl, 91
recitation, 26, 72, 188
redemptive history, 14, 49, 60, 66, 69, 135, 169
Reformation, 72
Reformed Orthodox Church, 39
Reformers, 5
regeneration, 56, 139
Renihan, James M., 160
resurrection
  of human beings, 172, 175, 184, 190–91, 194
  of Jesus Christ, 13, 98, 139–40, 144, 146, 148, 167, 169, 184, 190–91, 194
  theology of, 51, 172

revelation
  from acts in human history, 27, 34, 48, 50, 54, 58, 66, 107, 118, 134
  divine, 59
  general, 6
  progressive, 59, 65
  from Scripture, 27, 49, 54, 66, 103, 131, 154
  from Spirit, 134, 139–40, 149–50
Roman Catholicism, 142

S

salvation, 9, 34, 51, 56–58, 60–61, 65–68, 96, 98, 118, 121–22, 135, 139, 143–44, 150, 161, 163, 168–69, 173, 180–81, 183, 187, 191–94
sanctification, 18–19, 74, 128
Sanders, Fred, 50, 53, 106–7
Scripture
  authority of, 7, 55, 115, 185
  high view of, 7
  infallibility of, 55
  inspiration of, 27, 54, 66, 107, 185
  sufficiency of, 7
Second London Baptist Confession of Faith, 160
Shema, 78
Simply Trinity (Barrett), 3
sin, 13, 33, 37, 41, 43–44, 48, 59–60, 65, 116, 121, 123, 125–26, 133, 139, 147–48, 160, 184, 188, 190–92
Smith, Brandon D., 3, 145
Socinianism, 5, 115
Son. *See also* Jesus Christ; Word, divine
  begottenness of, 34, 36, 38–39, 56, 80, 83–88, 95, 102–4, 106, 108–12, 114, 117, 120, 122–23, 136, 140, 156, 158, 166, 183, 187, 190–94. *See also* filiation
  communion of believers with, 70, 140, 168
  equality with Father, 34–35, 83, 89, 94–95, 194
  eternal nature of, 13, 34, 62, 64, 122, 186
  eternal relation to Father, 35, 39, 80, 87–88, 99, 101–2, 112, 114, 155
  human nature of, 12–13, 93, 95, 117, 122, 136, 148, 162–63, 165, 176, 192, 194
  incarnation, 44
  intercession by, 86, 123, 132
  mission of, 63, 66, 95, 100, 121, 135, 163–64
  nature, divine, 33, 98, 149, 155, 163, 192, 194
  nature, human, 98, 194
  oneness with Father, 35
  person of, 64–65, 81, 98, 100–101, 106, 114, 117, 165–66, 176, 192, 194
  as power of God, 155
  procession of, 39, 114
  as truth, 149

union of believers with, 170
work of, 65, 98, 100, 126, 132, 169
soteriology, 51, 145
spiration, 39, 57, 81–83, 89, 107, 127, 136, 138, 143, 158, 183. *See also* Spirit: breathed out; Spirit: procession of
Spirit
   breathed out, 39, 81, 83, 120, 138–39, 141. *See also* spiration; Spirit: procession of
   as Comforter, 145, 170
   communion of believers with, 70, 168
   as Counselor, 133
   descent of, 66, 107, 132–33, 140
   divinity of, 128, 130–31
   equality with Father and Son, 83
   eternal relation of, 81, 127, 136, 138–41, 143–45
   as gift, 56, 59, 132, 137–41, 147
   indwelling by, 132, 148, 150
   intercession by, 129, 145–48
   as love, 136–37, 141, 155
   mind of, 145, 147
   mission of, 59, 66, 144
   outpouring of, 48, 53, 59, 61, 65–66, 107, 164–65
   person of, 56, 81, 107, 125–26, 130–31, 192
   power of, 126, 140, 145, 150, 169
   presence of, 133–34, 137, 157
   procession of, 37–39, 59, 81, 102, 108, 114, 120, 125–50, 156, 158, 165, 184, 191, 193. *See chapter 5, "The Lord and Life-Giver,"* (125–50); *see also* spiration; Spirit: breathed out
   work of, 18–19, 44, 125–26, 131, 134
Spurgeon, Charles, 46
subordinationists, 87
subsistence, modes of, 8, 38, 82, 95, 101, 156
subsisting relations, 82–83, 87, 90, 93
substance, divine. *See also homoousios*; essence, divine; nature, divine
   oneness of, 36, 38, 72, 79, 108–10, 114, 191
   simplicity of, 89
   of Son, 94, 99, 108, 110–12, 114, 122–23, 183, 191
   of Trinity, 74, 88
Summa Theologia (Aquinas), 161
Swain, Scott R., 3, 50, 61, 120

T

Tanner, Beth, 172
temple, the, 29, 86, 173–74
theologia, 34, 57, 159. *See* Trinity: ontological

theological methodology, 6, 13
theology
    Christian, 19, 21, 24, 49–50, 119, 180–81
    dogmatic, 4, 7, 15, 51
    historical, 7, 15
    natural, 6
    trinitarian, 15, 17–46, 50–51, 53, 110. *See chapter 1, "A Rediscovery"* (17–46); *see also* trinitarianism; Trinity: doctrine of
Three-in-One, 50, 144
Timothy (church leader), 186
Titus (church leader), 186
tradition, Christian, 1, 4–6, 20–21, 26, 54–55, 80–81, 90, 93, 109, 152, 170, 185–86
    authority of, 55, 185–86, 189
    of the East, 141
    pro-Nicene, 32, 94
    of the West, 141
transfiguration, 166
trinitarian formulas, 66
trinitarianism, 79, 104, 188. *See also* theology: trinitarian; Trinity: doctrine of
    classical, 1, 15, 117, 185
    orthodox, 7, 167
    pro-Nicene, 90
    social, 89–95
Trinity, 17
    agency of, 63
    communion with, 56, 69–70, 133, 151–77, 179. *See chapter 6, "Communion with the Undivided Trinity,"* (151–77)
    and creation, 31, 34–35, 40, 42, 57, 61, 64–65, 67–68, 76, 85–86, 91, 96, 107, 140, 151–52, 157, 161, 163, 168
    distinction within, 14, 31, 34, 38–39, 67, 79, 91, 95, 113–14, 120, 127, 141, 152, 154, 156, 159, 162, 164, 192
    doctrine of, 4–5, 13, 15, 17–46, 48–51, 53–55, 59, 67–68, 71, 113, 131, 167, 179–81. *See chapter 1, "A Rediscovery"* (17–46); *see also* theology: trinitarian; Trinitarianism
        classical theistic, 1–2, 182
        historic, 19
        load-bearing, 54
        orthodox, 1
    economic, 57, 91. *See also* Trinity: missions of
    economy of, 34, 57–58, 106, 114, 119, 123, 143, 159–61, 163. *See also ad intra*; *oikonomia*
    equality of, 9, 14, 40, 67, 79, 92, 95, 99, 159, 193
    essential properties of, 164–65

eternal nature of, 37–38, 40, 44, 50, 57–58, 61, 63, 67, 84–85, 89, 95, 125, 135, 160, 187, 193
eternal relations of, 14, 38, 50, 57, 66–67, 79, 83, 90, 102, 107, 115, 118, 120, 138, 156, 164
fellowship with, 123, 126, 150, 168. *See also* Trinity: communion with
immanent, 57, 91, 93. *See also* Trinity: ontological
indivisibility of, 8, 14, 38, 77, 79, 88, 96, 120, 123, 151–77, 192. *See chapter 6, "Communion with the Undivided Trinity,"* (151–77)
missions of, 14, 57–58, 68, 91, 107, 118–19, 164. *See also* Trinity: economic
mystery of, 8, 41, 56–58, 61, 68, 81, 181
and the Old Testament, 50, 54, 59–65, 104
oneness of, 9, 14, 17, 31, 36–38, 40, 44, 47, 50, 55, 61, 67, 71–96, 99, 102, 108, 113, 120, 132, 136, 138, 152–53, 156, 158–59, 162, 183, 187, 190, 192–93. *See chapter 3, "One God in Trinity"* (71–96)
ontological, 57. *See also* Trinity: immanent
personal properties of, 79–83, 87–88, 94, 102, 143, 164–65
persons of, 8, 12–14, 17, 33, 36, 38, 44, 50, 53–54, 62, 70, 72–74, 78–83, 89–93, 95–96, 99, 102, 105–7, 114, 118–20, 128, 132, 136, 151–52, 154, 156–59, 161–62, 165, 167–68, 192–93
processions of, 58, 80, 91, 103, 106, 118–20
self-existence of, 63, 65, 76
self-revelation of, 47–70, 131, 134, 176, *See chapter 2, "The Saving Trinity"* (47–70)
self-sufficiency of, 35, 76. *See also* aseity
transcendence of, 48, 57
unity of, 35, 37–38, 66–67, 69–74, 79, 81–82, 85–87, 90–91, 93, 96, 107, 112–13, 120, 139, 152–53, 179, 192–93. *See also* Trinity: oneness of
will of, 12, 34–35, 79, 85, 87, 90, 93–94, 117, 120, 136, 147, 153, 157–61, 164–66. *See also* centers of consciousness
works of, 60–62, 70, 118, 134, 154, 157, 160–62, 165–68, 175, 180

external, 14, 96, 120, 153, 177
Trinity, The (Swain), 3
tritheism, 79, 93–94, 154
triune life, 19, 44–45, 126, 180
Turretin, Francis, 63, 82, 94, 116, 161

U

"Ungratefulness" (Herbert), 41
univocal language, 135

W

Warfield, B. B., 60
Webster, John, 101
Westminster Confession, 49
Westminster Larger Catechism, 21–22
wisdom (divine attribute), 33, 35, 59, 111, 120, 125, 135, 145, 160
Wisdom, divine, 31, 34–35, 62
Wittman, Tyler R., 8, 159
woman at the well, Samaritan, 149
Word, divine, 31, 35, 40, 43, 61–65, 107, 111, 166, 192. *See also* Jesus Christ; Son
worship, 2, 38, 108, 119, 134, 139, 149–50, 175, 184, 191–93. *See also* liturgy

SCRIPTURE INDEX

Genesis
1:1 *53, 107, 151, 154*
1:1–3 *61–62*
3:8 *130*

Exodus
3 *63*
3:14 *63–64*
33–34 *64*
33:7 *64*
33:14 *64*
33:18 *174*
33:18–23 *170–71*
33:23 *64*
34:6 *64*
34:6–7 *63–64*
34:32–35 *64*

Leviticus
9 *22*
9:24 *22*
10 *23*
10:1 *23*
10:1–7 *22*
10:2 *23*

Numbers
6:22–27 *62*

Deuteronomy
4:35 *73*
6:4 *37–38, 50, 54, 78, 99*
6:5 *44, 78*

1 Samuel
19–31 *172*

2 Samuel
23:2–3 *62*

Job
19:26 *171*

Psalms
2 *61–62*
2:7 *104*
4:6 *130*
16:10 *12*
17 *171–73*
17:1 *171*
17:2 *172*

17:3 *172*
17:9 *171*
17:11 *171*
17:12 *171*
17:14 *171*
17:15 *171–75*
17:15b *172*
18:10 *130*
19:1 *40*
22 *11–12*
22:1 *11*
23 *12, 130*
23:4 *12*
23:6 *12*
24 *8–9, 13–14*
24:1–2 *10*
24:1–10 *10*
24:3 *10*
24:4 *10*
24:6–7 *9*
24:8 *11*
24:10 *11*
27:1 *173*
27:2 *173*
27:4 *29, 171, 173–76*
33:6 *40, 61, 63*
33:9 *61*
34:16 *130*
44:23 *130*
73:23–26 *52*
79:5 *130*
80:1 *130*
110 *61–62*
139:2 *53*
145:16 *130*

Proverbs
8 *34, 62, 104*
8:22 *34*
8:22–24 *31–32*
8:25 *34, 104*

Isaiah
5:25 *130*
24:23 *171*
33:17 *174*
37:16 *130*
49:3 *62*

Jeremiah
9:23–24 *23*
31:26 *130*
31:33 *126*

Micah
5:2–4 *62*

Matthew
2:15 *62*
3:17 *105*
10:20 *138*
11:27 *67, 105*
16:18 *20*
17:5 *105*
24:36–39 *105*
26:39 *154, 165*
27:46 *11, 154*
28:19 *50, 54, 67*

Mark
1:11 *105*
3:11 *105*
9:7 *105*
12:1–12 *63*
12:30 *98*
12:35–37 *62*

13:32 *98*

Luke
1:35 *167*
4:41 *105*
8:28 *105*
15 *116*
15:16 *116*
15:17–19 *116*
15:24 *116*
22:42 *148, 166*

John
1 *64*
1:1 *107*
1:1–3 *31, 62, 154*
1:1–14 *64*
1:3 *40*
1:14 *43, 64, 105, 167*
1:14–18 *64*
1:16 *64*
1:17–18 *64*
3 *136*
3:16 *104*
3:34 *137*
4 *137, 149*
4:23 *149*
4:24 *128–29*
5:17–19 *154*
5:19 *105*
5:22–23 *95*
5:26 *105, 110*
6:38 *118*
7 *137*
7:37 *98*
8 *104–5*
8:25 *104*
8:26 *104*
8:33 *104*
8:42 *105*
10 *87*
10:24 *86*
10:25–26 *86*
10:26–27 *86*
10:27–28 *87*
10:29–30 *87*
10:30 *34–35, 113*
10:31 *87*
10:32 *87*
10:33 *34, 87*
12–17 *131*
12:28 *154*
14:15–17 *133*
14:23 *133*
16 *131, 133*
16:7 *132*
16:8–11 *133*
16:12–13 *133*
16:14–15 *133*
17:6–26 *154*
19:30 *132*

Acts
2 *98*
2:1–4 *107*
2:38 *137*
5:3–4 *54*
10:45 *137*
13:33 *104*
17 *180*
17:28 *75, 180*

Romans
3:24–25 *123*
5 *137*
5:3–5 *137*

8 *145–46*
8:1 *148*
8:3 *167*
8:11 *148*
8:23 *146*
8:24–25 *146*
8:26 *129, 146*
8:26–27 *146, 148*
8:27 *147*
11 *69*
11:36 *97*

1 Corinthians
1:24 *59, 155*
2:10 *45*
2:10–12 *134*
4:7 *26*
8:4 *73*
8:4–6 *154*
8:5–6 *73*
8:6 *38, 54, 68, 127*
12–14 *137*
12:3 *67, 150*
12:4–6 *68*
13:9–11 *174*
13:12 *182*
13:13 *171*
14:15 *129*

2 Corinthians
3:12–4:6 *170*
3:18 *74, 182*
5:21 *97*
13:13 *67*

Galatians
3:8 *60*
3:16 *60*

4:4 *44, 66*
4:4–7 *59, 63, 68*
4:6 *123, 138*
5 *137*

Ephesians
1 *164*
1:4 *164*
2:1 *121*
4:4–6 *68*

Philippians
2:5–11 *30*
2:7 *95*
2:7–8 *95*
5:8 *95*

Colossians
1 *25*
1:9–10 *45*
1:9–12 *25*
1:9–14 *69*
1:10 *25*
1:15 *31–32*
1:15–18 *30, 154*
1:17 *41*
1:18 *97*

1 Timothy
1:17 *28*
1:18–19 *186*
4:16 *186*

Titus
1:9 *186*

Hebrews
1 *62, 104*

1:1–3 *154*
1:3 *97*
1:4 *97*
1:5 *104–5*
5:14 *186*
6:1–3 *49*
7:25 *123*
10:11–14 *123*
12 *97*
12:3 *97*
13:8 *109*

James
1:17 *xiv*

1 Peter
1:1–2 *18*

2 Peter
1:17 *105*

1 John
3:2 *171*
4:10 *105*

Jude
v. 3 *7, 26*
v. 5 *154*
vv. 20–21 *150*

Revelation
5 *10*
5:2–3 *10*
5:7–10 *10*
22:3–5 *174*
22:17 *150*